The POWER Series

US MARINE CORPS

Hans Halberstadt

Motorbooks International
Publishers & Wholesalers

First published in 1993 by Motorbooks International Publishers & Wholesalers, PO Box 2, 729 Prospect Avenue, Osceola, WI 54020 USA

Library of Congress Cataloging-in-Publication Data

Halberstadt, Hans.
    US Marine Corps / Hans Halberstadt.
        p.   cm. — (The Power series)
    Includes index.
    ISBN 0-87938-769-6
    1. United States. Marine Corps. I. Title. II.
    Series: Power series (Osceola, Wis.)
VE23.H29 1993
359.9'6'0973—dc20   93-13163

Printed and bound in Hong Kong

On the front cover: The Marine Corps eagle, globe, and anchor.

On the back cover: Top, a Marine Corps F/A-18 Hornet. Bottom, Marines are tough because they are trained by the toughest drill instuctors in any service.

On the frontispiece: The Marine Corps has made a tradition of never leaving its fallen on the battlefield. This painting depicts a bayonet charge by the men of Bravo Company, 1/26 Marines, who assaulted North Vietnamese positions outside the Marine perimeter at Khe Sahn on March 30, 1968, to bring back the dead from a Bravo Company patrol that had been ambushed. Painting by Kevin Lyles. Prints of this image can be obtained from Kevin Lyles, 24 Victoria Road, Birkhamstead, Herts, HP4 2JT, England.

On the title page: This platoon of recruits participate in a ritual older than the United States. Drill once was an important part of the command and control system that allowed commanders to influence battle. Now it teaches discipline, teamwork, and attention to detail and provides a link with the past.

Contents

Dedication

To the ladies! And particularly to Mrs. Suzy Sullivan—one of the most lady-like ladies of them all—bride of Col William R. Sullivan, captured in the Marine Corps campaign in New Zealand during 1942, veteran of many Marine Corps expeditions, one Marines' personal "force service support," and a living example of Corps values.

Acknowledgments

This project is largely the fault of my friend and neighbor Capt Greg Mast, USCMR, who has been prevailed upon numerous times for help with obscure bits of Corps trivia, anecdotes and diverse intel support. Refer all criticisms to him, care of the publisher's S-2 shop.

Many thanks to the Marines, past and present, who supported the mission (in approximate order of appearance): CWO Randy Gaddo, Col Fred Peck, MGen Joseph P. Hoar, Lt Kevin Bentley, "Top" Farrell, Capt Dave Bonner, Capt Ralph Mills, Capt Greg Glasser, LCpl Adrianne Fossegan, Maj Doug Hughes, Lt Mike Scalise, Lt Col Robert E. (Bob) Lee, Capt Bob Chase, GySgt Dave Billinovich, SSgt Courtney, and a multitude of others who assisted with the project. Thanks also to the Public Affairs shops at Yuma, Cherry Point, Camp Pendleton, Twentynine Palms, and Headquarters USMC.

And a salute to Sara Saetre, my blue-pencil-pal, minder of my p's and q's, for spit-shining the manuscript to a high gloss.

Chapter 1

Receiving the Mission

The United States Marine Corps is a curious institution. Of the four American armed forces it is the smallest, with about 165,000 people on active duty, only 10 percent of the Department of Defense. Despite the small numbers it has a huge responsibility. It has missions that seem to duplicate elements of the bigger services and sometimes looks like parts of the Army, the Air Force, or the Navy. Marines fight on the ground, like the Army. They use fighters to achieve air superiority and to attack ground targets, like the Air Force and the Navy. Marines serve aboard ships, as do sailors, and are considered an essential part of the Navy. Marines use many of the same weapons, uniforms, vehicles, aircraft, language, procedures, insignia, and all the other institutional components as the Army, Navy, and Air Force. From the outside, at first glance, Marines look like other services—but that impression is an illusion. The United States Marine Corps is a very unusual and utterly unique little community, with its own special character, its own set of responsibilities, and a huge legend based on a record of accomplishment, bought with blood, unequaled by its larger sister services.

They used to say the Corps built men—what they meant was that it developed men (and now women) into people with exceptional character, upon whom the nation places exceptional trust.

The Marine Corps is, in many ways, a lot less like a government institution than a religious order; take away the guns and uniforms and it can sometimes be difficult to tell a Marine from a Jesuit. Both offer themselves in service to the larger community. Nobody expects to get rich in either. Military communities—the good ones, anyway—and religious orders both tend to trade heavily in ritual, symbolism, sacrifice, and ceremony; ethics are a large part of the philosophy of both kinds of communities. In fact, both institutions often measure the achievement of individuals by their suffering and tolerance of adversity. Jesuits don't get tattoos or (usually) swear as articulately as Marines but the dedication to mission and to community are often equally intense.

The Corps used to say that it built men, but what the slogan meant was that it built *character*. There is something about the way Marines are selected and developed that not only produces character, it produces *characters*. People join the Army, Navy, and Air Force essentially to get a job and when the job is over those people are out of the institution in every way. The Marine Corps, by contrast, is a calling that offers and demands much more of an applicant, rather like the Jesuits or Franciscans, and most people who survive boot camp consider themselves Marines for the rest of their lives. The Army offers job training, adventure, good pay, and travel—the invitation to "be all you can be" approach to service. Jesuits and Marines offer a challenge, a mission, an opportunity for service and sacrifice and suffering for the very few special people who are called and chosen. Both are extremely selective. Both place high demands on the individual. The result of both programs is a person with a special sense of self and institution that lasts for a lifetime. You can join the Army—or you can be a Marine. Within the community of American armed services, Marines are unique again because most will candidly and cheerfully admit that they love the Corps.

In fact, Marines are encouraged to be unique in many ways; they are the only branch of the armed forces that retain the sword for officers and sergeants. They are unique in cultivating an appreciation of their history, a major part of the instruction for new officers and enlisted people. Marines, alone among the services, have a reading list of books for all ranks to study and discuss. They, alone among American forces, have managed to develop their community into a kind of cult religion, part private and part public. No other American unit has such gaudy uniforms, such affection for parades and public display of glittering swords and banners, and ranks of tailored dress blue uniforms. It is the only one that really demands a heavy commitment from new recruits, and those recruits are trained longer, harder, and to a higher standard than any other entry-level program. And,

In a dozen ways, Marines insulate themselves from civilian society—with uniforms, rituals, traditions, standards of behavior—in ways that resemble those of religious orders.

of all the services, the Marine Corps is the only one that attains life-time loyalty from its members; as they say, "once a Marine, always a Marine."

The Marine Corps was born, (appropriately) in a tavern, on the tenth of November, 1775. For the first twenty years of its existence it was just like the marine forces of all the other navies of the time. It was a police force for the sailors aboard ship who were, even then, quite likely to mutiny, jump ship, or abandon their guns in battle. Marines of all navies were stationed in the rigging of ships in battle to fire muskets down on the opposing crews. And when there was plunder or glory to be had ashore, it was this sea-going infantry that climbed into the flimsy little ship's boats and rowed to the beach with musket and saber. In this, the United States version of the marine force was essentially like that of Great

The noncommissioned officers of the Corps have produced many of its heroes over the years; they train both new officer candidates and new privates, inspiring both in the process. This DI (as drill instructors are known) has been selected and trained to pass on all the many values and virtues of the institution.

Marine sergeants have their own version of the sword, used on special occasions. This staff sergeant is preparing for a graduation parade; he practices along with the recruits he has supervised for the past twelve weeks and helped to convert from civilians to Marines.

Britain (after which it was patterned) only smaller, less skilled, worse equipped, and with an even worse officer corps—if that was possible.

Now, it could easily have been that this little Marine Corps could have long faded from the organization chart of government, a little footnote in the history of American institutions. But there is something about certain military institutions that defies logic, where a community somehow acquires for itself a special character that makes it larger than life. And that's what happened to the Marine Corps. If you've never been a member of the Marines, or the Russian Spetsnaz, or one of Britain's fabled regiments like the Coldstream Guards it can be difficult to appreciate that some communities develop into profoundly spiritual institutions. It is one of the fates and fortunes of war that sometimes groups of people find themselves inspired by the same events that destroy others. That transformation is the one thing that can't be bought, as can the weapons and equipment, and can't be imposed by a government. It just happens or it doesn't. For the United States Marine Corps it began to happen twenty years after the Corps was born, on 27 April 1805 when one Marine officer and seven enlisted Marines executed an operation that set the standard for audacity and valor that have served the Corps all these years

Lt Presley Nevil O'Bannon on the Shores of Tripoli

In the years after the Revolution the United States was a small, isolated, defenseless nation with an active maritime trade. Like other, bigger, nations, one of the costs of doing business at the time was the risk of piracy—and that cost could sometimes be quite high. Piracy was the growth industry of the time, and most commercial shipping carried large numbers of cannon to deal with them. The pirates tended to carry even more cannon and were often a match for even the naval vessels of the day. It was accepted, for a time, as unavoidable, but in 1805 the United States, in cooperation with several other nations, decided after several extreme provocations that the pirates operating in the Mediterranean had gone too far.

An expedition was assembled to attack the pirate stronghold in Derna. The cast of characters assembled looked like something out of one of the "Indiana Jones" epics, with Arab and European mercenaries, eight scrawny US Marines, a few visionaries and lunatics, and not much more—a total of about 500 men, an assortment of mules, and an undisclosed number of camp followers. Up front was a US Army general, William Eaton, a diplomatic agent who had put the whole force together, with the Marines included for glue.

The whole mob was put ashore at Alexandria, Egypt, about 600 miles from the objective, the fortress city of Derna in what is now Libya. After chasing around North Africa for a few weeks in search of political support, the force finally started moving across the 600 miles of desert toward the objective—on foot. Along the way there were mutinies and occasional disorder, murders, dissension, desertions, all suppressed by the little corps of Marines. Finally the force closed on the fortress city of Derna and prepared to attack.

The assault began on the morning of the 27 April 1805. Off shore the naval guns of the task force bombarded the fortress city while the ground combat element attacked through the gates and into the city. With bullets whizzing, the Marines dashed for the big guns of the fortress, fighting all the way with musket and saber. Arab coalition forces took one side of the defenses, the tiny American Marine force another. The guns were seized and turned on the enemy headquarters. For two hours they pounded the building with the enemy's own big guns while the naval force off shore attacked the same target.

The fight was brief, violent, successful; after several hours the enemy commanders capitulated and the bulk of the enemy force fled the fortress, running for the open desert, pursued by part of the force while the rest consolidated on the objective. The Marines stayed in the city, and the lieutenant, a young man called Presley Neville O'Bannon, accepted the surrender of the enemy commander. He had lost two Marines killed and one wounded; the entire coalition force had lost a total of thirteen battle deaths. That battle was the first example of power projection and the protection of sea lanes by the young United States and the first time the American flag was hoisted in the Old World.

That combat set the standard for Marines from then forward—in more ways than one. The act of this tiny unit achieved results all out of proportion to their numbers. They achieved their victory through incredible audacity and against impossible odds. They took tremendously high losses: about 40 percent casualties and 25 percent killed in action. But instead of destroying the pirate organization, the victory was squandered by the naval task force commander. O'Bannon and his Marines were briefly a media sensation back in the United States, but they received no medals or promotions for their accomplishment. Marines have become accustomed to such results; it has become another part of the tradition.

O'Bannon did get one reward, although it wasn't from his countrymen. In fact, it was from the enemy commandeer who gave the young officer a sword. That weapon, called the Mameluke sword, became the pattern for the one still carried on ceremonial occasions by all Marine officers. And although O'Bannon didn't get formal honors at the time, his leadership and accomplishment inspired the Corps and his memory is well preserved and loved. As one lieutenant remarked, he became the pattern and inspiration for young Marine officers, the role model for the breed. In a way, the Marine Corps was born at Derna through the valor of one scrawny young officer, one sergeant, and six Marine riflemen.

Character and Characters

Adversity can either strengthen or break people and institutions. Somehow it has strengthened both Marines and the Marine Corps whose enemies have managed to be

"What Marine earned five Navy Crosses? Tell me which two Marines each earned two Medals of Honor. What is your First General Order?" This first sergeant participates in a battalion commander's inspection, a last evaluation of each recruit. The recruits' knowledge of a thousand details is tested, their weapons inspected for traces of carbon on the operating handle, and the fit of their new Class A uniforms is evaluated.

both foreign and domestic—including several of its own commanders-in-chief. Andrew Jackson was the first president to propose its elimination and tried to dispose of it in 1829; after World War II, Harry Truman did the same. Instead of being killed off, the Corps has thrived, defeated its adversaries (on and off the battlefield) and evolved into today's little band of brothers and sisters with a global mission. Perhaps it has been the constant challenges from within the American armed forces community and government, along with the battlefield mission traditionally assigned to Marines that has tempered and strengthened the people and the institution that we call the Corps. Whatever the reason, the result has been a profound one.

While not everybody thinks Marines are the best in the force-projection business, there is no debate about the shape and character of

The Mameluke sword is owned by every Marine officer and used fairly often for ceremonial occasions, particularly the Corps Birthday on November 10. It is patterned after the one presented to Lt Presley O'Bannon in 1805. It is a beautiful weapon that was used in combat as recently as 1931 in Haiti; at least one Marine officer carried his on operations in Vietnam, but apparently he was unable to skewer any Viet Cong with it.

the Corps or its journeymen. Marines are held to a higher standard than members of other American military communities in several important ways: in their initial selection, in their initiation into the Corps as officers or as enlisted Marines, and in their physical fitness and battlefield performance. Their training lasts longer (twelve weeks for boot camp as opposed to eight for Army basic training), demands performance to a higher standard. And on the battlefield Marines have a tradition that requires success, at any cost. As one Marine says, "We are different from the other services—we must never lose a battle."

Marines, in peace and war, experience adversity. Boot camp is hard with extreme levels of stress applied from the moment the recruit arrives. Officer training is harder, longer, with an attrition rate that approximates 50 percent. Life in the rifle companies demands very high levels of physical fitness and tactical proficiency. Marines routinely spend six-month periods jammed aboard ships, away from homes and families, on deployments they call "floats." When war comes, as it regularly does, Marines seem to bleed more than the other services. In places like Belleau Wood, Guadalcanal, Tarawa, Peleliu, Chosin Reservoir, and hundreds of others before and after, Marines have accomplished great things at great cost. The process seems to have built an institution that grows heroes.

O'Bannon was the first; the only honor he got from his exploit was a sword and the admiration of Marines down the years. But there have been many others who've inspired and amazed Marines. Smedley Butler who was commissioned an officer at age sixteen, fought in the Banana Wars and won two Medals of Honor in the process. He tried to turn one down, but had to keep it anyway. He was known as "Old Gimlet Eye" and was the kind of Marine who would (and did) chase an enemy commander down and drag him from his horse.

Dan Daly was another winner of two Medals of Honor, one on the wall at Peking, China, where he held a crucial outpost alone, under fire, and another one in Haiti where he retrieved a vital machine gun—again, under fire. And later, as a "gunny" it was Daly who, in the battle for the Belleau Wood, led his Marines into a murderous German fire with the question, "Come on you sons-of-bitches, do you want to live forever?"

"Chesty" Puller is another Marine hero who rose through the ranks from private to lieutenant general, winning five Navy Crosses in the process. As a young lieutenant in El Salvador he led a little patrol that fought four battles in ten days; later he distinguished himself on Guadalcanal, Peleliu, and especially in Korea. There Puller commanded the incredible fighting withdrawal from Chosin Reservoir, one of the epic battles of the Corps. Something about Puller's character caught the imagination of his Marines. He seemed, then and now, to have become the embodiment of what Marines call Semper Fi, a kind of bulldog determination in the face of adversity, an unwillingness to quit, to surrender to anything or anybody. Not only did Puller bring his Marine dead out from Chosin with him, he brought the vehicles and weapons that he'd been ordered to abandon, too—and he destroyed nine enemy divisions in the process of withdrawing. It was another of those performances that set the standard for what a Marine leader should be and do.

Commandants all manage to achieve hero status, at least to the younger, starry-eyed Marine officers and enlisted personnel. Archibald Henderson held the slot for thirty-nine years, from 1820 to 1859; he died in office at the age of seventy-six. Since then, commandants have had to move on a lot more often, but they all achieve a kind of god-like role during and after their tenure "on point."

From the example of these Marines and many others has evolved a kind of code of conduct called "Corps values" that defines the standard of performance expected of every single Marine at all times and places. It is a profoundly moral standard based on a kind of love Marines have for each other and their society. For example, Marines never abandon

The Corps demands performance to a high standard—in everything, at all times, of every man or woman who wants to be a Marine.

their wounded or dead on the battlefield; they must be recovered, at any cost. Marine officers in the field eat only after their men have been fed; if there isn't enough chow (and sometimes there isn't) the officer goes hungry. On the Navy's ships, by contrast, officers are served by their sailors, dressed up in waiter outfits—a tradition that disgusts many Marine officers.

The Marine Corps, more than any other American force, cherishes its heroes—worships them while alive and preserves their memories when they die. Marines study the history of their battles and the people who fought them, particularly the ones like O'Bannon who have an audacity that seems particularly Marine.

The Corps has always been a small world, where people know and remember each other. You can hardly go on any major combined-arms exercise (CAX) without bumping into people you've met or worked with at Quantico, Okinawa, Parris Island, or on a Western Pacific (WESTPAC) "float." There are familiar faces (and reputations) everywhere in this big family. It is the kind of place where a kind of auda-

15

cious character has become more than just acceptable, it has become expected in individuals, particularly by the time they become gunnery sergeants ("gunnys") or captains. The Marine Corps, in other words, is full of living legends and dead heroes, equally beloved. As one officer commented, that may be because throughout the history of the Corps it has been the sergeants and corporals who've had to summon the self-confidence to take over in combat and complete a mission when all the officers have been killed or wounded.

The character of Marines is different than that of other service members. Part of it is a kind of brash courage, like that of O'Bannon, in the face of long odds. Part of it is a strong sense of community that Marines have with other Marines, condensed into an attitude expressed as Semper Fi. That contraction of the Marine motto, Semper Fidelis ("Always Faithful") has been adapted to summarize a kind of special bond and brotherhood Marines feel for each other. As one officer observes, almost every Marine will freely admit that he or she loves the Corps. Almost all (including old veterans of distant wars) sign their correspondence Semper Fi. And, as another officer points out, you can be in the Army, Navy, or Air Force; you are a Marine for life.

This intensity and affection for the Corps results in all kinds of demonstrations of affection. For example, one Marine lost an eye in

Adversity develops a perverse sense of humor, as well as character. This Marine has applied his "cammy" in a bulls-eye pattern.

Vietnam, and the glass one that replaced it has, instead of an artificial pupil, the emblem of the United States Marine Corps.

Marine Mission—Past

When the Corps was formed back in 1775 the mission of American Marines was designed to be exactly the same as the marine forces of France and England and all other naval powers. First, Marines were needed to keep the sailors aboard in line—a kind of seagoing police force. Mutiny at the time was quite common, the result of extremely low recruiting standards for sailors, extremely bad living conditions aboard ship, and often abusive and incompetent officers. The Marine complement aboard ship was considerably more dependable and disciplined and could be called on to suppress the occasional uprising. This was particularly important when a combatant vessel closed with an enemy and engaged because now the sailors' living conditions were even worse, what with cannon balls tearing up the living spaces and enemy boarders trying to slice up the crew with cutlasses. Marines encouraged the sailors to stick to

"In every place and clime . . ." includes winter cruises to vacation spots like Norway and a chance to enjoy *all sorts of snow sports: cross-country travel, digging snow forts, and fighting with the locals.* USMC

their guns by essentially not giving them any choice in the matter. Second, Marines were stationed during battle on platforms on the ships' mast where they could fire down on the enemy. Their musket fire could clear the exposed deck of an enemy ship, with luck killing or disabling the enemy commander should he be so brazen to expose himself to the fire (and many were). At extremely close quarters Marines tossed grenades down on the enemy ship, aiming for the hatches in the hope of getting at the enemy's gunpowder supplies. When the ships finally grated together in a hostile embrace, Marines were the first across the rail to fight the enemy sailors and marines. Finally, when there was a need to go ashore and fight, Marines were the first choice. Sailors usually accompanied them in the ship's small boat. Using muskets and cutlasses they were supposed to assault the objective. (And they usually did, too, although sometimes not before stopping at a tavern for refreshment first).

Marine Mission—Present

The mission for the Corps has evolved from those original missions into a responsibility to provide an independent, expeditionary, naval, combined-arms, task–organized force whose mission is to seize advanced naval bases and to conduct land operations related to a naval campaign. Secondarily, the Corps coordinates planning and doctrine for amphibious operations. And, like the other services, ". . . other duties as the President may direct."

The "independent" part of the mission has been a sore point until recently. President Truman attempted to have the role of the Corps reduced or eliminated after World War II. Truman endorsed a plan, designed by the Army, to unify the armed services into one Department of War with a single chief of staff. The idea created much debate and serious consideration, and ultimately led to the conversion of the old Department of War, until World War II housed in one moderately sized office building, into the mammoth Department of

Defense headquartered in the Pentagon. The Army, Navy, and the newly created Air Force all had secure roles in the new department, but the Marine Corps, as ever, was without a place at the table. When a member of congress wrote Truman to encourage better use of the Marines, Truman expressed his attitude about the Corps:

"The Marine Corps is the Navy's police force and as long as I am President that is what it will remain. They have a propaganda machine almost the equal of Stalin's . . . The Chief of Naval Operations is the Chief of Staff of the Navy of which the Marines are a part."

The response was tremendous when the comments were reproduced in the newspapers. Marine loyalists were outraged. Although Truman didn't retract the remarks, he attended the Marine Corps League dinner the day after the remarks appeared in the papers.

Perhaps as a result of Truman's hostility, congress protected and defined the role for Marines within the Department of Defense. The mission for the Corps today is to be a single, integrated combined-arms combat organization, the Marine Air-Ground Task Force (MAGTF). The expression "combined arms" means a mix of infantry, artillery, armor, aviation, and supporting elements into an effective and versatile force. Combined arms is a World War II development, brought to a fine art by the Germans and enthusiastically adopted by American and British armies. When used intelligently, it allows a single commander to always put heat on an enemy with one kind of weapon or another. The Army also uses a combined-arms model, but its organization is less flexible than the way Marines task-organize and its missions are more diverse.

Mission Elements
Expeditionary role

This MAGTF is an expeditionary organization particularly designed for amphibious assaults and sustained operations. "Expeditionary" means that the Corps has the assignment to travel quickly to distant places, deal with almost any kind of emergency; it means being very flexible, mobile, agile, and still carrying enough firepower and groceries to complete the assignment. Marines expect to go off to distant shores and bleed on them; that's the tradition and the mission. Although O'Bannon wouldn't have called it that, he led the first task force ashore in the Old World, a Marine Expeditionary Unit (MEU) with many of the elements of any modern assault. As small and as simple as that little expeditionary force was, it defined the mission for Marines pretty well—it projected combat power across the globe, across the beach, hit the enemy with a combined-arms task force (ground and naval gunfire support), all in a triumph of tactical and logistic planning. It was what's called a "high risk, high payoff" operation, and it succeeded largely because of the character of those few Marines and the support they got from the Navy.

Army units, even though they may wear identical uniforms and use identical weapons, are normally strategically immobile, tied to a particular piece of ground, in Europe or Korea, with a limited mission and a limited range of tactical options. Army divisions can be moved, but it isn't usually easy, and it isn't pretty—except for the light-infantry and airborne divisions whose mission is to be ready to travel with an eighteen-hour notice. They are expeditionary too, but with far smaller missions and resources.

So the combat elements of the Corps have a kind of unique role in the armed forces—they have to be a global force, ready to go anywhere, to fight and win. They have to be both agile and powerful, with heavy combat power when they arrive. That is one of the classic problems of warfare—how to "get there first with the most." It has never been easy, but that's the mission. As one Marine explains:

"Because of the proximity of oceans to populated areas around the world, we can land in an undefended area, conduct our operations ashore, strike at the critical "point of balance" of the enemy and defeat him quickly. It allows us a lot of flexibility. Systems like the LCAC

Expeditionary means travel, a lot of it in the Pacific. The Corps is configured to put a lot of combat power and the supplies to sustain it on any beach that might be necessary, a potent weapon and perhaps the most important one in the uncertain future.

19

[Landing Craft, Air Cushion] and "vertical envelopment" allow us to strike the heart of the enemy.

Unified Command

When Army, Navy, and Air Force units work together, in exercises or in real world operations, chaos frequently rears its ugly head. Marines call this kind of confusion a "goatscrew." That's because the different services have often ignored the capabilities and limitations of the others, because the radios used by the Army's tanks and infantry could not talk to the Air Force's fighters overhead or the Navy's gunfire support ships offshore.

Marines, by contrast, are designed to be a single, integrated team; it's called "playing off the same sheet of music" and the conductor is the Marine officer who commands the MAGTF. He's in charge of the whole mix of forces: air superiority over the beach, the landing team that goes across it, the close air support and artillery that protects the assault, the logistics "tail" that follows and sustains it. Having a single commander solves many of

The eagle, globe, and anchor symbolize the Corps' image of its mission: force projection, based on sea power, with a global commitment.

the problems that have defeated combat units throughout history.

Sustainable

When the United States began to hit back at the Japanese in World War II, in August of 1942, it was on the steamy island of Guadalcanal. The Marine assault force got ashore against minimal opposition but was abandoned by the naval transports before the supplies and equipment were on the beach. The Japanese counterattacked against a weak and vulnerable Marine task force that survived only by eating captured rice, using captured weapons and equipment, and by doing a lot of bleeding. The experience taught a lot of lessons, one of which was that putting an assault force on the beach was only the beginning of the battle and that keeping it there was sometimes the hard part.

Marines still don't let their Navy colleagues forget Guadalcanal, and the concept of amphibious operations ever since has put heavy stress on avoiding another experience like that. So Marine operations are built around complete packages of ammunition, food, water, and medical supplies that follow the assault elements ashore. The smallest task force carries two weeks worth of supplies with it, the largest carries two months worth. As one officer explains:

"We land very 'heavy.' We land with thirty days' supplies. It may take us a while to get there—longer than an airborne unit—but when we land we've got food, we've got ammo. In fact, we fed the 82nd Airborne in Saudi."

Integrated Ground-Air team

The commander of a MAGTF is both a composer and a conductor; he writes the score and coordinates the orchestra during the performance. A lesson learned from every conflict since 1941 (and particularly on Guadalcanal) has been that it takes a combination of effective air units and ground units working on a single plan to ensure success on the battlefield. Marine doctrine emphasizes this relationship by insisting on an "organic" air force of its own, under the command and control of

The first wave comes ashore. Normally (the fates and fortunes of war permitting) this is done under cover of night, but this daylight rehearsal shows how it is done. These are AAV-7s (Armored Assault Vehicles), big, lightly armored amphibious vehicles that can carry twenty-five Marines (if they are small ones, and on friendly terms) ashore and then take them inland. It can do seven miles per hour in the water, forty-five miles per hour ashore, and has a range of 300 miles.

the commander of the landing force (the CLF, pronounced *cliff*) who has both a ground combat element (GCE) and air combat element (ACE) to work with.

Combined Arms

All Marine units are part of what is called the Fleet Marine Forces, a combination of the Navy's ability to transport, support, and sustain a combat operation ashore. The Marine component includes four parts: 1) a ground combat element, with infantry, armor, artillery, engineer units—usually called the GCE; 2) an air combat element, called the ACE, with squadrons dedicated to air superiority, close air support, and combat service support; 3) a command and control element that plans, controls, and directs combat operations; 4) a service support group that provides the essential supplies and services that keep the operation going for days, weeks, or months.

Task Organized

One of the lessons learned from World War II was that flexibility helped win battles. The British and Germans early developed custom-designed groups of forces for specific missions. They would carve a company of tanks out of a tank battalion and send them off with

The Corps' ultimate weapon isn't the Hornet fighter or the Abrams tank. It's the young Marine with the M16A2 rifle who can "hump" a rucksack twenty miles in a day and put a bullet in a man-sized target at 300 meters.

a battalion of infantry, perhaps with a battery or two of artillery from yet another unit. It worked much better than the previous method of employing forces that kept the units "pure." After the operation was completed the components reverted to their parent commands. It was an efficient, effective technique that let a commander mix and match resources. For some tactical problems you will want to use a lot of infantry but support it with, for example, some armor and perhaps artillery. On the other hand, an armor unit often needs the support of infantry. A commander plans an operation based on the mission and the resources at hand. A fundamental of Marine doctrine is that forces are organized for the task at hand, not as a permanent unit. These task forces are usually custom designed for an operation. They come in small, medium, and large sizes.

Security

Just about the oldest mission Marines have is to police Naval vessels and it is something they still do. That's why the guard outside a carrier captain's stateroom will be a Marine, and so too will usually be the guards of nuclear weapons and powerplants.

Marines likewise provide some of the security duties ashore for naval installations, providing gate guards and patrolling the base—as well as the adjoining watering holes frequented by sometimes rowdy sailors and Marines. The Marine Security Battalion is tasked with responsibility for the most sensitive sites (nuclear weapons storage, for example) and as a kind of SWAT team for security emergencies within the naval establishment.

Other missions

The Corps gets tapped for a lot of little activities that could be done by any of the services but that are trusted instead to just the Marine Corps. Marine helicopters transport the president and Marine sentries guard the White House. Marines guard many US embassies around the world.

Structure of the Corps

The Marine Corps is an on-call reaction force, ready to deal with emergencies that threaten American interests worldwide. It works with the Navy, which can deliver large volumes of people and weapons and the supplies to sustain both fairly quickly and to very distant locations. It is not alone in this mission, but Marines are dedicated to putting a particular kind of serious force ashore nearly anywhere it is needed.

Now, there is some competition about this rapid-reaction role. The Army's 82nd Airborne Division, in concert with the Air Force, claims that it is the premier quick reaction force. The 82nd maintains a brigade on alert status at all times, with vehicles, weapons, ammunition, and people ready for "insertion" into a hostile air head by parachute or by being "air landed." This brigade, called the Division Ready Brigade, or DRB, is constantly prepared to plan, mount, and execute combat operations worldwide—with the first aircraft "wheels up" no more than eighteen hours from notification. That's fast, faster than the Marine Corps. Those paratrooper's can be on the ground in a combat zone in Grenada or Panama or the Persian Gulf area only hours later. And, if not used very carefully, they can all be dead a few hours after that.

The 82nd Airborne and the Marine Corps actually complement each other in the rapid deployment role. The airborne is a light-infantry organization, designed for brief, fairly low risk combat operations against an opposing force that is lacking much armor. The 82nd packs a quick, light punch. It owns no real tanks, has little armor or anti-armor capability, not much artillery or organic close air support. It is vulnerable to tanks, and to the passage of time because it brings very little "sustainability" along. If not reinforced within forty-eight hours the 82nd will be in deep trouble. It is a light-infantry force, with all the virtues and vices of that kind of organization.

The Marine Corps, by contrast, is a heavy combined-arms force that takes longer to arrive but normally puts a much heavier force on the objective. It is a less stealthy assault, but a more powerful one. Marines come across the beach with at least a couple of weeks sup-

Capt Dave Bonner and one of Marine Air Group (MAG) 32's night-attack variants of the AV-8 Harrier. MAG 32, based at Cherry Point, North Carolina, sent Captain Bonner and a lot of other Marines to the Gulf for the recent unpleasantness. Instead of close-air-support missions supporting Marines in heavy contact with enemy infantry, the Harriers were called on to perform more deep-air-support missions against Iraqi transportation and communication facilities, troop concentrations, artillery, and armor parks. Like every other Marine, Captain Bonner is expected to be a competent rifleman in addition to his primary assignment.

ply of food, water, ammunition, and spare parts. A Marine assault also comes complete with all the tanks and light armor, artillery and organic close air support a commander could ask for. But the Navy/Marine version of the script is biased heavily to "force projection" that could be launched from the sea. Of course, since so much of the earth (70 percent) is covered with water, there is a pretty good possibility that an amphibious operation will be suitable for a crisis, but there are also plenty of places where the nearest beach is thousands of miles away and an airborne operation is the only option. There is a time and place for both kinds of operation, light and heavy, and recent events have shown that both usually end up being employed in the same fight, as in Normandy in 1944 and in the Gulf in 1991.

Although the uniforms and most of the weapons, and even, in a way, the people start out as essentially the same for all the services, the Marine Corps adapts all to a unique community. The Army has its divisions, its brigades, and its regiments, but they are all quite different than those of the Marines. The Army's brigades are dedicated, permanent organizations with a history and a mission, as are Marine regiments, but there are some fundamental differences.

Fleet Marine Forces

There are two parent organizations for all operational MAGTFs with the unwieldy names of Fleet Marine Force Atlantic (FMFLANT) and Fleet Marine Force Pacific (FMFPAC), one facing the Atlantic and the other the Pacific. These FMFs "own" the forces within their limits: the 2nd Marine Division in the case of FMFlant and the 1st and 3rd Marine Divisions for FMFpac.

The vast Pacific has traditionally been a busy place for Marines, and FMFpac, headquartered at Camp Smith, Hawaii, uses two of the three Marine divisions to patrol it. One of these is 1st Marine Division, based at Camp Pendleton, California, that maintains I Marine Expeditionary Force (MEF) at Twenty-nine Palms. FMFPAC also operates III MEF and the 3rd Marine Division, based on Okinawa. Both divisions always have elements deployed on "floats," ready to respond to crises. FMFPAC has an area of interest that occupies nearly half the globe and has the lion's share of Marine operational forces worldwide.

The FMFlant is headquartered at Norfolk and is responsible for 2nd Marine Division, headquartered at Camp Lejeune, North Carolina, plus the 2nd Marine Air Wing at Cherry Point, North Carolina, and the 2nd Force Service Support Group also at Camp Lejeune. They maintain a continuous presence in the Mediterranean, conducting frequent training amphibious assaults on both sides of the Atlantic. Both these "parent" organizations are responsible for forces and missions around the world, rather like the administration of a huge fire department.

Maritime Pre-Positioning Ships

After the American role in the war in Southeast Asia concluded the United States underwent a massive reconsideration of its role in world events and the role of the individual armed forces in whatever new policy evolved. Despite the traditional pressures for an isolated, uninvolved America, the decision to remain a player on the stage was made. One of the events that influenced the decision was the Yom Kippur War; a decision to support Israel's defense against the Arab armies turned out to be very difficult to fulfill. Then came the Iranian hostage crisis and the botched rescue attempt. It became obvious that the strategic lift capability of the nation was badly lacking and that huge numbers of personnel and weapons were useless if they couldn't be delivered to the combat zone in a timely way. The bean counters started looking at just how many C-5 and C-141 sorties would be required to put a serious force on top of a crisis and discovered that the lift just wasn't there. Worse, it wasn't going to ever be there: the costs were just prohibitive.

The solution turned out to be to use the transport aircraft mostly for personnel and critical cargo and to store the heavy equipment and supplies needed by an expeditionary force aboard ships all the time—and to keep the ships out close to where the action is or might be. That's the Maritime Pre-Positioning concept, and it works like a charm.

There are thirteen Maritime Pre-Positioning Ships (MPS) ships, all huge and all designed for the job of supporting a Marine task force. Four MPS ships can carry all the vehicles, weapons, supplies, ammunition, and all the other travel accessories required by a Marine Expeditionary Brigade (MEB) for thirty days, the equivalent of 249 sorties by Air Force cargo aircraft and sufficient for about 16,500 Marines. A typical MPS vessel can carry about 1,400 vehicles, 100,000 cubic feet of general cargo, 230,000 cubic feet of ammunition, 1.5 million gallons of fuels, and 80,000 gallons of drinking water. The ships can travel at around nineteen knots and have a range of about 12,000 miles (half way around the world on a tank of oil). Each comes with its own landing craft and causeways, its own tug, and its own three-mile hoses for dispensing fuel direct to the beach.

When Kuwait was invaded on 8 August 1990, a squadron of MPS, the *Anderson*, *Bonnyman*, and *Hague*, (known officially as MPSRON-2) were close by at the island of Diego Garcia. They were under way about the same time the 7th Marines received their warning order, just hours after the invasion. The main body of the 7th Marines—the 7th MEB—from Twentynine Palms started arriving aboard USAF C-141s on 15 August, eight days after notification. They were "married" to their equipment immediately because the MPS system delivered them exactly as advertised. The MEB included about 17,000 Marines who took over tanks, trucks, Light Armored Vehicles (LAVs), M109 self-propelled guns, artillery, anti-armor missile systems, hospitals, and all the other combat assets required to field a credible combat force, and within days they formed a hard core around which the buildup continued. The Army's 82nd Airborne arrived first, only about a day and a half after receiving their order, but was only strong enough for securing the airfields until more help could arrive. The Marines, by contrast, took about a week to show up but were conducting combat patrols and preparing to defend against an armored assault within days of arrival.

The Regimental System

The names and relationships of military organizations can bewilder a newcomer to the subject not familiar with the idea of regiments, brigades, battalions, and companies. But these are extremely important notions within military organizations because each is like a tribe, with families and kinship relationships nesting one within another. Inside the big, 160,000 man-and-woman Corps are four divisions, each containing several regiments and groups; each regiment and group contains battalions; the battalions are assembled from companies. And each company has its platoons built from squads and fire teams, all assembled from individual Marines.

A regiment, in the traditional sense, is at least two (usually three) battalions, each battalion having at least two (usually three) companies of troops; that works out to about 1,200 people. A Marine infantry regiment will have three infantry battalions plus supporting units. Each of these battalions will have at

You can't fight without logistics support, one of the four elements of a task force. Here comes some logistics support now, high-explosive projectiles for the 155mm guns.

least three infantry companies. A regiment's 1st Battalion will always have A, B, C, and sometimes D companies. Second Battalion will always have E, F, G, and sometimes H companies. Third Battalion will then always have I, K, L, and sometimes J and M companies. An infantry rifleman in either service will think of his battalion as his "home." If he's a member of the 82nd Airborne, he could say he's from the "First of the Three-Two-Five" meaning the 1st Battalion of the 325th Parachute Infantry Regiment. A Marine will say, for example, he's from "First Battalion, Ninth Marines," or "One-Nine," never "First of the Ninth," as does the Army.

Unfortunately, the Army applies the term "brigade" to this regimental organization, while the Marines use the term for a particular kind of expeditionary task force. It is confusing. Not only that, but the Army is returning to the long-neglected regimental system, and has both regiments and brigades running around loose at the same time, with the same kinds of assets. An Army brigade is three battalions—infantry, armor, artillery, or aviation—each battalion containing three companies of about 125 people, plus supporting units that bring its strength to about 2,000 soldiers. Army brigades come in standard flavors: infantry, artillery, armor, and are quite permanent.

A Marine brigade only exists as a temporary MAGTF and is a complete, all-arms organization much more like an Army division. The Marine version has about 16,000 people, with lots of organic aviation, armor, artillery, infantry, and supporting logistics units. In fact, this Marine brigade is larger than most Army divisions, and is far more capable of sustained combat operations. There are only two MEBs presently activated, 1st and 9th; 4th and 5th "stood down" in the summer of 1992.

Navy Support

The Navy's contribution to the Marine mission often gets slighted, although not by Marines themselves. The Navy dedicates a lot of resources, money, and people to amphibious assault. There are five classes of amphibious force ships, including a specialized aircraft carrier, the *Tarawa*-class amphibious assault ship, plus the Landing Ship, Dock (LSDs) of the *Whidbey Island* class and others. Without them there would be no amphibious assault or logistic support.

Ships like the *Tarawa* essentially replace three vessels of earlier years. They form the heart of the amphibious operation, with 1,700 Marines aboard and facilities for thirty-five aircraft. The *Tarawa*-class ships also launch and recover Landing Craft, Air Cushion (LCACs) and Armored Assault Vehicles (AAVs) from its well deck. CH-46 Sea Knight helicopters can launch assault elements from the little carriers' deck and carry Marines right over the beach defenses to seize key terrain from the rear rather than the front.

And LSD vessels like the *Whidbey Island* and *Germantown* are designed primarily to do nothing but support Marine operations. They have flight decks that will accommodate a helicopter or two, but their primary mission is to put vehicles on the beach. To do that the LSDs have room for four LCACs, each of which can carry about six or so LAVs, High-Mobility Multipurpose Wheeled Vehicles (HMMWVs, known simply as Humvees) or other light vehicles, or an M1A1 Abrams tank. The LCACs add an entirely new dimension to amphibious assault with their big payload and tremendous speed. They will come ripping across the ocean at better than fifty miles per hour. They don't need to be launched close to the beach like AAVs or previous landing craft but can come over the horizon if need be. With a range of about 350 miles on a tank of gas, the LCACs can come ashore almost anywhere. The air cushion system lets the LCAC come across the beach in places that previously were impossible—and which were consequently undefended. It will hover right across swamps, sand dunes, mud flats, and tidal inlets to find a suitable spot to deposit its passengers. Tides, beach gradients, underwater obstacles, and water depth (things that drove World War II planners crazy) are suddenly non-issues because the LCAC just floats over them.

If LCACs make things easier for the assault force, they must drive the defenders to distraction. Only about 17 percent of the world's shoreline is suitable to receive a conventional beach landing but about 70 percent will receive an LCAC. And with the versatility of the helicopter assault added to the LCACs and AAVs the problem of defending a shoreline against an attack by United States Marines becomes extremely difficult and expensive, if not practically impossible.

The Future of the Corps

The Corps has survived against all odds and in spite of the best efforts of several presi-dents and numerous legislators. The same old agitation to get rid of the Marines, one way or another, is still present and the Corps' existence is still subject to challenge. At this writing the Corps is undergoing one of its ritual shrinking acts, with famous and fabled units disappearing from the rolls.

One of the reasons has been that its mission has always looked suspiciously like that of the Army's . . . when its missions have been defined at all.

It's a component of the Department of the Navy—but it is also a co-equal member of the armed forces. Many of its missions overlap those performed by the Army, Air Force, and

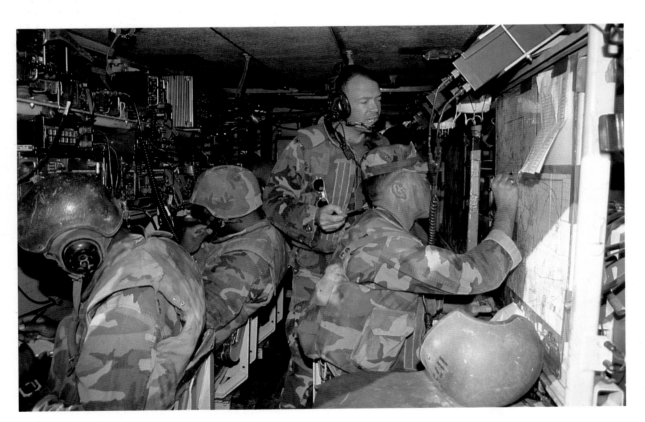

Command and control. The control in this case is being exercised by Capt John Kinney, the fire support coordinator for 3rd Battalion, 9th Marines.

Chapter 2

The Making of a Marine

About 40,000 young men and women sign contracts every year pledging themselves to the Corps. The typical prospective Marine is a high school graduate, nineteen years old, single, and male. Many have college experience, and some new recruits have college degrees. About 4 percent are women. The testing process begins with the recruiter who must compete with the other services for new enlistees. Unlike the Army, Navy, and Air Force, Marine recruiters don't normally stress job training, good pay, travel, educational benefits, or adventure. Instead, they tend to offer a challenge and a possibility of membership in an elite military organization. As one Marine officer who rose from the ranks explains, "The Army recruiter promised me all sorts of opportunities, and the Air Force recruiter did the same. When I got to the Marine Corps recruiter I asked him what the Marine Corps could offer me. He looked at me for a minute and said, 'Nothing, son. What can *you* give the Marine Corps?' I joined the Marines. The Marine Corps tends to attract overachievers and misfits—somewhat like the French Foreign Legion. I was seventeen, five-foot-five and a

At the end of a demanding twelve-week training cycle, a young recruit waits to be inspected by his company commander. If found acceptable, he will be allowed to graduate and only then will he be called a Marine.

hundred and twenty-five pounds when I enlisted; nobody thought I'd make it through recruit training, but I graduated in the top 10 percent of the class."

Another officer who also served a hitch as an enlisted Marine explains, "The difference between the Marines and other services' initial training is that you're expected to give a lot more than you get. It's kind of a monastic experience, an emphasis on service and sacrifice. It's 'the Marine Corps never owes you anything—you always owe the Marine Corps.' It's not a nine-to-five experience. You don't take off the haircut at the end of the day."

The recruiter begins the screening and selection process. It takes a lot of time and effort to find, test, evaluate, and ship off a prospect to the induction center where the physicals are done. All prospective recruits go through a process that measures their suitability for the rigors of recruit training and life in the Corps. Intelligence is tested with the National Armed Services Vocational Aptitude Battery; most accepted for the Marines score above average on the test. Police records are investigated; any problems with the law must be minor.

Two recruit depots provide basic training—the fabled Boot Camp. One is at Parris Island, South Carolina, for recruits from east of the Mississippi and all women recruits; the other is at San Diego, serving those from the west. Each depot receives about 20,000 recruits each year. The two depots use the same

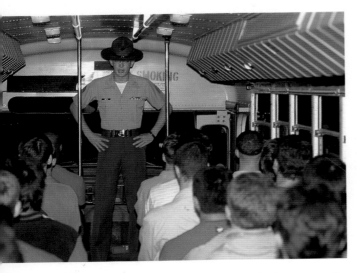

Sergeant Smith welcomes a busload of new recruits to the hospitality of Marine Corps Recruit Depot San Diego.

"Now—the first thing you will learn is the position of attention." One busload of fresh privates begin the long process that will ultimately make most of them Marines.

program, but there are still differences in the experience. Parris Island is a long bus ride from the nearest airport, across a waterway allegedly filled with alligators hungry for absent-without-leave (AWOL) recruits. Once on the island there is a feeling of isolation and remoteness that can be quite powerful. About the only thing visible for the new recruits are trees and drill instructors, the DIs of legend.

San Diego, on the other hand, is directly adjacent to a large, busy city. Evidence of civilization is everywhere—particularly when one of the big jets takes off every few minutes, the only noise on earth that is louder than a DI. (To compensate, the recruits are often instructed to fight the jet noise with shouts of their own; entire training companies roar their defiance at every departing aircraft). San Diego lacks alligators but is overrun by hordes of cottontail rabbits—"killer bunnies" as they are called by the inmates. Marine Corps Recruit Depot (MCRD) San Diego's proximity to civilization, just across the fence, affects new recruits in different ways: some find the nearby city reassuring, while for others it just in-

creases the loneliness for a young man away from home and family for the first time.

New recruits usually travel by commercial airline, individually or in groups, and are met by young, perfect sergeants on arrival at the airport. They are put on busses and delivered to the reception building, normally in the evening, to begin in-processing. Until this moment, each recruit has been treated with a certain amount of civility by the recruiter and the personnel at the induction center. That stops when the DI climbs aboard the bus and gives the new recruits their first order and starts the process of turning these quivering, undisciplined, raw chunks of humanity into Marines.

It is not an easy job. Lesson One is delivered by a tall, slender sergeant who is scarcely older than the recruits about to enter his custody. His uniform is perfectly tailored, immaculate in every detail. Away from the recruits, the sergeant is relaxed and amusing company, an intelligent and enthusiastic young man—until the bus rolls to a stop. The smile evaporates. The door to the bus opens and he steps purposefully aboard to welcome the new recruits to the hospitality of the depot. He personifies every virtue and high standard of the Corps. Eyes glittering from just below the DI hat, he tells the new privates in a voice that crackles with authority:

"You are now aboard MCRD—Marine Corps Recruit Depot receiving barracks, building 622. From now on, the last words out of your mouth at all times will be 'sir;' is that understood?"

"YES, SIR!" the new privates roar, if they are smart. No matter how loud they are, it won't be loud enough.

"I said, IS THAT UNDERSTOOD?"

"YES, SIR!" they roar, even louder.

"When I tell you to get off my bus, you are gonna stand up, you are going to form a single-file line, and you are going to get on the yellow foot-prints starting from front to rear and from left to right. Now, look down around you and pick up anything you brought with you and put it in your left hand. Now, at this time, without running, pushing, or shoving, STAND UP, FORM A SINGLE-FILE LINE, AND GET OFF MY BUS!"

They scramble off as fast as they can, suppressing panic and the desire to run. Several DIs are waiting like vultures. They pounce, yelling: "QUICKLY! QUICKLY! HURRY UP!

The kindly, attentive staff of well-trained DIs is ever alert to the smallest need of the young men in their care during their visit to San Diego or lovely Parris Island. They dedicate countless hours to guiding the new privates through the exciting and educational experiences to be enjoyed at Marine Recruit Depot, carefully watching each and every one to make sure that no opportunity for personal growth and enrichment is missed. Each friendly, considerate DI generously offers helpful hints, suggestions, guidance, and instruction in the military arts ensuring an exciting, rewarding experience that each is sure to remember.

Raw material for the DIs. About one in ten will be sent home, disappointed.

HURRY UP! HURRY UP! WALK! WALK QUICKLY!"

The learning process starts immediately with the position of attention. The new recruits quickly learn that they don't even know how to stand up properly, but the kindly, attentive DI soon has each of them approximating the correct position of attention, Marine style: heels together, feet at a forty-five–degree angle, shoulders back, thumbs aligned with the trouser seam, eyes to the front. No smiling, no talking, no kidding. "IS THAT CLEAR?"

Lesson Two for the new recruits is an introduction to the Uniform Code of Military Justice, the law that applies to all members of the armed forces, including new ones. It quickly becomes apparent to all that the normal protections and procedures for civilian wrongdoing have been modified for the needs of the military. Article 15 authorizes a commanding officer to be both judge and jury; Article 86 describes the crime of absent without leave, and Article 92 the requirement for obedience to lawful orders. And Article 124 covers just about anything else by requiring good conduct,

order, and discipline. The bottom line for the new recruits is obvious: they are at the mercy of the system and they had better be extra careful to be nice.

About this time, one or two may begin to cry. Many will have sudden, intense doubts

Quite a different young man than the civilian that climbed off the bus three months previously—tougher mentally and physically, a team player and maybe beginning to learn how to lead, a manager of time and stress, and he knows how to clean up his room and make his bed, stand up straight, and he now says "yes sir" instead of "yeah." No wonder the mothers cry when their babies are finally Marines.

How different, really, are these young men from their ancestor Marines of 1812 or 1775?

about the wisdom of the decision they've made. It doesn't matter. For the rest of the night they will be standing at attention, attending classes, receiving their initial clothing issue. Within the first hour of arrival, most will receive the famous haircut, a process that takes about twenty seconds, although the record is supposed to be five.

They will be issued a sweatshirt and one pair of pants. All connection with civilian life is stripped away, and what's left looks and usually feels pathetic, tired, and ugly. There is no respite from the pressure. Each recruit quickly comes to feel that the DIs can see every character fault and flaw, that each is under constant scrutiny. A feeling of inadequacy results in extreme sensitivity to all instructions. It continues through the night, right through the following day until evening chow. About 1800 hours (still known as 6:00 pm to most of the new privates) they will be allowed to fall into a bunk and sleep. Welcome to the Marine Corps!

This introduction is intended to be—and is—a profound shock. Most recruits have never been held to a really high standard for anything in their lives. No one has ever told them that they must do something perfectly— even something as simple as standing in one place or saying yes or no. The DI will not strike a recruit (as was once the case), but the effect of his or her verbal ire can be as devastating. Some attempt to quit and a few of these are sent home if they are really unsalvageable. It isn't uncommon for an occasional young man to bawl like a baby after the DIs begin to work their magic. And some will attempt escape, but the nearby airport is not much of a refuge for somebody with no hair, a sweatshirt with numbers on it, and camouflage trousers; they are promptly identified and collected by the security staff and returned to the depot.

One of the first things the recruits learn is that they are *not* Marines, and won't be until they graduate at the end of the training. Boot camp lasts twelve weeks and is divided into three stages. The first lasts four weeks and is designed to convert a young, out of shape civilian into the beginnings of a Marine recruit— the most difficult part of the process. The DIs begin that process on the bus and all during that first day by demanding a higher standard of performance in every activity. Phase One develops physical and mental discipline and teamwork and starts the physical training process. There is daily physical training (PT): warm up and flexibility exercises, push-ups, sit-ups, running. Most of the recruits have been sedentary; the PT routine starts out at a fairly reasonable pace, then escalates. Almost all of the recruits discover aches and pains but manage to get through the program.

A few can't keep up on the runs or complete the minimums for pull-ups or other exercises; they will either improve enough to meet

By the twelfth week, these recruits have picked up a few tricks: nobody is asleep when the lights come on—they are all just waiting to pop out of bed and into ranks, standing at attention just seconds after reveille. That must take some of the fun out of it for the DIs who stand around yelling, "GET UP, GET UP, COME ON, LET'S GO! OUT OF THOSE RACKS!" In about five seconds the entire platoon is standing at attention, ready to start another day.

35

No longer civilians, not yet Marines, these young men have come a long way. It seems odd to people who haven't experienced it, but this process that seems to rob people of their individuality actually encourages it. Each of these people knows far more about himself than he did when he got off the bus. He has discovered mental and physical strengths his civilian contemporaries mostly lack. An extraordinary number of Marines become high achievers in business and government, and a great many recall their boot camp experience with great affection.

the standard or they get to go to the Physical Conditioning Platoon where the chubby ones will be introduced to the USMC quick-weight-loss program, and where the ones who are just plain weak will be introduced to the joys of weight lifting.

During Weeks One, Two, Three, and Four, the raw recruits are introduced to close-order drill, they run the obstacle course, circuit course, and confidence course and get water-survival training. They get classroom instruction on Marine Corps history, first aid, customs, and courtesy (how to salute and when, whom to salute and why), the code of conduct, military law, and are introduced to the Rifle, M16A2, caliber 5.56mm. They will practice everything for hours. They will carry a thick

textbook everywhere and be expected to know everything within. People who have never really studied anything in twelve years of school learn to memorize a thousand details. Young men and women who were never interested in history classes suddenly know about the War of 1812, the battle of Belleau Wood, Tarawa, and Chosin Reservoir. Ones who were never interested in math suddenly know the effective ranges of a dozen weapons. People who never really had to work at anything now work hard at everything, all day and into the night.

Although the first few days of boot camp are typically highly stressful and sometimes frightening, over the following days and weeks the process succeeds at developing tremendous confidence and self-discipline. Most recruits have never been held to a high standard for anything in their lives; they, like their contemporaries, have been allowed to "skate" through life by indulgent and tolerant families and schools. But boot camp's Phase One demands that each individual becomes alert, attentive, physically fit, a team player. As the aches and pains subside and the distance of the runs increase, as the fumbles and awkwardness in close-order drill are replaced with precision, there is a kind of transformation in the recruits. For most of them, this is the first time in their lives they've ever accomplished something important—and the process becomes quite exciting.

During the first month of training the new privates must wear their Battle Dress Uniforms (BDUs) in a non-standard way, with the top shirt button fastened and the pant cuffs unbloused. This, the DIs say, will prevent onlookers from confusing the new privates with a real recruit. It looks awkward and ugly—as it is supposed to—and it is a major milestone in boot camp when, after the first phase is complete, the privates are allowed to wear the uniform like other Marines, with trousers bloused, sleeves rolled, and shirt collar open at the neck.

Phase Two is dedicated to training in basic infantry skills and with weapons, particularly with the M16A2. Week Five deals with weapons safety and basic marksmanship skills. Week Six is spent on the range, firing; each recruit fires for qualification, the best will be able to wear the coveted Expert badge on dress uniforms. Weeks Seven and Eight introduce the recruits to camping and backpacking, Marine-style: land navigation, field living, tactical movement techniques, plus survival techniques on the nuclear, biological, and chemical-weapon (NBC) battlefield. They get to throw a hand grenade and learn to employ Claymore mines. They are introduced to anti-armor weapons like the AT-4. Recruits discover the virtues and characteristics of the M249 Squad Automatic Weapon (SAW). They learn how to wear and use their combat load-carrying-equipment and how to refer to it as "782-gear" or "duce-gear." And they get to carry everything on long road marches—the last one for San Diego recruits being ten miles, including an uphill stretch called the "grim reaper."

Survivors go on to Phase Three. The recruits begin to see light at the end of the tunnel. After another month they will become Marines. They are only now issued the glorious dress blue uniform. The final weeks are filled with more PT, hand-to-hand and pugil-stick combat training, bayonet training, rappelling, tests, and inspections. After twelve weeks, about 10 percent of the recruits who started the process will have failed and have been sent home. The rest put on the tailored blue dress uniforms and parade before their DIs, officers, friends, and families—and can for the first time be called Marines.

Officers

While enlisted Marines tend to think of boot camp as a kind of ultimate test, that's only because they haven't been to the Officer Candidate Course (OCC), Platoon Leader Course (PLC), or the Naval Academy. These programs produce Marine officers, each of whom is supposed to be a kind of super Marine, able to lead by personal example. The standards for acceptance and survival in these officer programs is far more stringent than

boot camp—a program that must seem like an inviting few weeks of vacation for officer candidates.

As one survivor explains the process, "The mission of OCC is not to train you to be a Marine Corps infantry platoon leader; you are not going to come out of that program knowing how to deploy weapons systems. They are there to evaluate you and to train you to be a Marine. It was an experience I'll never forget. It was REALLY tough."

While the other armed services may teach job skills useful in civilian life, Marine recruits study the Rifle, M16A2, in the most minute detail, and the proper and approved ways of using it to kill people.

Another says about the process, "They started with a civilian—me—with a lot of grandiose expectations about becoming a Marine—all of which ultimately came true! But first they had to take this package of undisciplined material, this THING called an 'officer candidate,' and turn it into a Marine *officer*. They start with basics; they shave your head. You learn about basic weapons systems, customs and courtesies, Marine history (especially Presley O'Bannon), basic tactics—and more than anything, integrity and leadership."

There are essentially three variations to the process of commissioning officers. OCC is for college graduates or enlisted Marines and PLC is for people still in college; both are commissioning programs that last only a couple of months. Annapolis grads already have the gold bars of a 2nd lieutenant (entry level rank for officers) after four years in the Naval Academy but are not considered qualified to lead Marines until they've attended part of OCC called the Bulldog Program.

Unlike the commissioning programs for the other services, the Corps splits the process of developing officers into two parts. The first (OCC and PLC) involves a selection and evaluation process that really doesn't train candidates but rather puts them under stress to see how they respond. People who deal with the stress effectively and demonstrate leadership talent, intelligence, integrity, physical endurance, initiative, and teamwork skills earn a commission as a 2nd lieutenant of Marines. It takes ten weeks. Then they go on to learn the practical skills required of Marine officers at the second phase of the program at the Basic School, a twenty-three–week program that maintains the pressure in different ways.

OCC begins with about 250 people, most raw civilians with bad habits. Approximately 10 percent are women who are now fully inte-

Hand-to-hand combat teaches many useful skills that can come in handy in later life—how to break an elbow, throw and disable an opponent—just the thing for those pushy salesmen or rowdy board meetings.

grated into the training process, receiving exactly the same instruction on weapons and tactics, carrying the same loads the same distance as the men.

Men and women are now assigned to integrated platoons and companies and the women are required, by their instructors and peers, to meet the same standard as the men. Many seem to have risen to the challenge; one recent female candidate scored 295 on the men's physical fitness test (PFT), much better than the norm for any Marine, and many are able to execute proper pull-ups and push-ups. They now fight with pugil sticks and boxing gloves, just as the men do. And they are all subject to the same (often brutal) peer evaluation. A lot of Marines like the idea of full integration—as long as the standards for the women are the same as for the men. As one senior non-commissioned officer (NCO—a sergeant) says, "I really like the idea that women are training exactly the same way the men are. They earn the same pay—they ought to do the same work!"

About half of those who think they want to be Marine officers fail—but they don't get to quit until the sixth week. That's because the process makes just about everybody want to quit. It is a program that tests the resolve of everyone who experiences it. The last thing the Marine Corps needs in combat, in a leader or a follower, is a quitter. So at first the candidates don't have the option; after the sixth week they discover that they don't have the desire anymore.

Those who survive endure a kind of pressure that is designed to test their resolve. It is impossible to avoid failure in OCC. Every error that can be made will be made, sooner or later by someone in a class. Much of the program is administered by young Marine NCOs who appear to enjoy developing and testing odd forms of torture. And it seems that they are watching each candidate 24 hours a day, looking for the slightest error.

Part of the stress involves time management. A candidate is given a set of requirements that must be accomplished and then

Recruits learn early that the most stylish haircut in the Corps doesn't need blow-drying or gel. ✓

given insufficient time to accomplish the mission. This forces the candidate to decide what is the most and least important, to select just how much compromise with perfection is possible. They get thirty hours of work to get done every day. As one explains, "You've gotta be in the rack by 2100—but there's no way you can get everything done, so you've got to stay up until 0100 or 0200, ironing uniforms and studying for tests. And, this is after lights out so you do it by flashlight, under your blanket. If they catch you at it, you're going to get nailed."

Another part of the stress is strictly physical. Fairly early in the training, the officer-candidates run a nine-mile course in boots, full 60-pound packs, helmet, and with their rifles and 782 gear. "That helmet is the thing that kicks your butt," said one survivor. During the run are short excursions for various obstacle courses like the log roll. Then, at the end of the nine miles, the candidates immediately go through a reaction course that requires them to make tactical decisions while physically exhausted. You're graded on everything—your time on the run as well as the soundness of your decisions. One of the candidates says about it, "The stress is physical more than mental. The physical load becomes the filter; just how badly do you want that commission? How tired are you going to allow yourself to become, to be pushed? They call OCC the PT capital of the world. Sleep deprivation is part of it, too. One of the biggest mistakes you can make is thinking that OCC will get you in shape. You *go* to OCC in shape, or you're toast!"

The attrition rate is high, often about 50 percent. Candidates are lost for a variety of reasons. Some are injured, others can't hack the academics, others have trouble with the leadership skills. A few get cut for integrity violations. But the result is an officer who has

been trained and tested to an extremely high standard. A Marine officer leads by personal example. The result of the whole process is to produce a leader/follower relationship that can be quite strong and affectionate, in both directions, despite the traditional gulf between officers and enlisted personnel. As one officer says, "We are very close to our Marines, in the field and in garrison—more so, I think, than the other services are with their enlisted people.

"At the core of our existence are the history and traditions of the Marine Corps, passed on from generation to generation. Part of the reason for our success on the battlefield is an unwillingness to let that heritage down. During the Gulf war we were getting letters from

Battalion commander's inspection, but the company commander is checking them out first. And while the captain makes an adjustment of an almost-Ma-

rine's uniform, the platoon sergeant sends the next recruit a wordless yet eloquent message of warning. ✓

guys who'd been in the company during Vietnam and Korea, who didn't know anybody in the unit, asking how we were doing, asking about Lima Company. Each battalion has a history, a legacy, a heritage from previous battles, previous wars. It's a key to the way we work. That was my greatest experience—it doesn't get any better than to be a company commander of Marines in war."

The Basic School

All new Marine officers go directly to the Basic School (TBS), also located at Quantico, Virginia, in the piney woods south of Washington DC. Quantico is often called "the crossroads of the Corps" because all officers spend time there, and it is at the many schools and programs on this installation that relationships are built and developed that last for whole careers.

OCC and PLC select people able to lead Marines; TBS teaches them how. Despite what some Marines will tell you, TBS doesn't actually stand for "thousands being stupid," "taxes being squandered," "time between Saturdays" or "the bozo show;" this is where acolyte officers come to learn their trade. This program takes a raw Marine "butter bar" (as

This young man is two days away from graduation and achieving full membership in the Corps. He will put on his tailored dress blue uniform, form up on the parade deck, stand in formation for hours, then finally pass in review and be called, for the first time a Marine. He is stronger mentally and physically, transformed in many ways from the person who stepped off the bus more than three months ago. But that is still two days away and there is still more drill, classroom instruction, and inspections.

Entry-level officers wear the gold bar of a second lieutenant. While "butter-bars" take a lot of friendly abuse for their "Lt Fuzz" reputation, each one has survived a grueling selection and training process.

41

Bob Chase was an enlisted Marine for years, and a staff sergeant, when he finally applied to the Officer Candidate Course; he's now a major, the operations officer (S-3, they're called) for 3rd Battalion, 9th Marines. Such officers are called "mustangs" and bring to the leadership business a special insight that the enlisted Marines often appreciate.

the owner of the gold insignia of a 2nd lieutenant is sometimes called) and turns him or her into the officer who knows what to do, when, and how—in and out of combat.

TBS lasts twenty-three weeks. It includes a lot of work on tactics and combat leadership skills. The students learn about the planning process: how to receive an operation order, how to prepare orders for subordinates, and how to cope with a wide variety of tactical problems. The student officers take turns in every job in a platoon and company. Each gets a chance to command the unit, to be the executive officer, to command a platoon, a squad, a fire team, and to play the role of a rifleman, a SAW gunner, and a grenadier. The process is designed to give each officer an insight into the problems and potential of each role. They learn that time flies faster when you have planning and preparation to do; they learn how heavy the base plate for the mortar is after a few miles of a road march; they learn about their own talents for command and leadership. TBS concludes with a nine-day war. The students have to plan and execute

When an officer finally gets to pin on the silver eagles of a full "bird" colonel he or she becomes a member of a very select community. Colonel Stanley commands the 7th Marine Regiment.

Lt. Davelle Ann Yergey, 1st Marine Division's Protocol Officer.

Many Marine officers consider the time spent as a company commander (normally as a captain) the most pleasurable and rewarding of an entire career—no matter what may follow.

This is an era of uncertainty for many officers. As the mission of the Corps is reevaluated and adjusted to a changing world and the size of the institution is shrunk, many officers are being forced to consider civilian careers.

operations, move across long distances, attack, and defend.

When TBS finally concludes, the young lieutenants will be both officers and qualified to lead Marines. There is now specialist training and a career-long professional development and study process that will keep the officer qualified to lead. As an operations officer from a Marine regiment explains:

"You go into battle aware that your Marines are going to take care of you.

"You aren't afraid of death or of getting wounded so much as the horror of letting the other Marines on your left and right down. It isn't the enemy so much as that 217-year-old tradition of the Corps. People expect a lot from us—and we expect more from each other. *That's* the difference between us and the other services.

"We lead by example—on EVERYTHING. We eat last, to make sure our Marines are fed. Our appearance, our physical fitness, our knowledge of weapons and tactics—you can't *lead* if you can't do it. I have to be more proficient, better cross-trained. It is my obligation to the command and the Corps."

Chapter 3

Command and Control:
How Operations are Designed and Executed

The Corps thinks of itself as a single weapon with four moving parts. The parts are the ground element, the air element, the support element, and the command element. The weapon doesn't work if any of the parts are missing. And of all the parts, the part that has traditionally been most important is that of the commander and his staff. The pages of military history books are littered with the stories of brave and well-armed armies wasted by poor commanders and staff planning errors. The Iraqi army was just the latest of these—equipped with modern weapons in profusion, staffed by many thousands of soldiers, all foolishly used.

Command and control involves, in essence, spending the lives of Marines to achieve some national goal that justifies the cost. Although it hasn't happened recently, there have been many operations in the past where the cost was staggering, as at Iwo Jima where entire companies were used up, one after another, to slowly abrade the Japanese defenders in their bunkers and pillboxes. The slaughter happened because Marine commanders had no

practical choice but to send people they knew and genuinely loved to certain death. It is the sort of thing that can, and has, driven many a commander berserk.

When Marines and the rest of the planning staff that designed Desert Storm huddled over the maps and sand tables, designing their offensive operations to liberate Kuwait, they expected something like Iwo Jima might occur. That it didn't was partially the result of luck, partly enemy incompetence, and also a result of an excellent system of command and control.

Since nothing can be done about the "fates and fortunes of war" and very little about enemy competence, a commander makes sure his operations are planned with tremendous care and concern. Although the commander has the responsibility for the operation, it will be planned by a large congregation of officers and NCOs.

When the plan finally gets written it will trickle down the chain of command to the Marines who will execute it. The standard format for any operation is actually quite simple—a good thing, considering how easy it is for things to get ugly in combat. The format is used throughout all of NATO (and maybe the Russian Army, for that matter) and is known universally as the Five Paragraph Field Order. When it starts out at a MEF headquarters, the order can be pretty technical, with plenty of amendments and overlays, but as it

Unsung heroes, the infantry has been the traditional battle winners for the Corps. This young Marine has the dubious honor of "humping" the big 81mm mortar tube in addition to his other equipment. Somebody else gets to carry the base plate, and the whole squad will each carry some ammunition.

45

gets down to the individual battalions, squadrons, batteries, platoons, and finally squads it becomes more and more elegant and to the point. Here's how it works:

The MEF or MEB will generate an Operation Order that will be based on five classes of information:

Situation: first, the enemy's, then friendly forces, plus any attachments and sometimes the commander's personal assessment.

Mission: what is supposed to be accomplished.

Execution: the tactical plan to accomplish the mission, including scheme-of-maneuver,

fire support; each of the units in the command will be told what role they play in the operation.

Service support: where the ammo, water, transportation, evacuation of casualties and prisoners comes from.

Command and signal: radio procedures, where the commander will be during the operation.

The planning process will finally reach the company and platoon commanders. They get their orders, receive their maps, schedules, recon photos, intel briefings, radio frequencies, and call signs. There is an ancient ritual to

Command and control means that everybody "plays off the same sheet of music"—or, in this case, sand table.

this performance, most of which is presented by the senior operations officer. His staff will have designed the details of the mission, based on the intentions of both the Marine CLF and the Navy CATF (Commander Amphibious Task Force). Here's what the operations officer sounds like:

"Our mission, commencing at H-hour on D day: Regimental Landing Team FIVE is to secure Objective Bravo and effect a link up with Army airborne forces vicinity ATF Alpha in order to deny the enemy access to the beach area and to secure a lodgment for MPS off load and follow-on operations.

"Concept of operations: at H-hour the First of the Five Oh First air drops into DZ Basilone. Approximately five hundred soldiers will be dropped from C-130 aircraft flying at 800 feet AGL.

"Team Shepherd, our focus of effort, lands via LCAC at White Beach, prepare to take Landing Force Objective Two, link up with the Army at ATF Alpha and with the absence of the Army they will take ATF Alpha. Second Battalion, Third Marines, lands at Red Beach, take ATF Objective Bravo. First Battalion, Fifth Marines, helicopter-borne, on call; their possible mission is the airfield, Landing Force Objective One.

"Commander's intent: to provide a variety of tactical looks, to promote confusion and ambiguity for the enemy.

"The focus must be a rapid link-up with Army forces, to rapidly project combat power ashore and *not* follow the beach, but to attack the enemy's critical vulnerability—extended lines of communication, his inability to communicate, and his lack of mobility . . . "

Orders like the one above are crafted by a small, essential group of Marines—both officer and enlisted—who staff the headquarters units. Despite what the folks in the rifle companies think, the people who try to manage the chaos of a Marine division do not actually bring champagne and a portable hot tub to the field with them. The rumor about the color TV is a lie, and so is the one about the ice cream every night. The one about the coffee pot in the S-2 track is, however, true.

An infantry battalion will get a "warning order" well in advance of an operation that alerts everybody to prepare for a mission. The warning order is typically very simple, vague, and occasionally wrong but serves the purpose to get people packed and ready to move, even if they end up moving in a different direction. The battalion commander and his "orders group" will go off to receive their mission from the regiment. All the other battalion commanders will be present and all will receive their order at the same time, a great way to keep people "playing off the same sheet of music," as they say.

When the battalion commander returns with his order, he and his staff huddle and prepare their own op order. The commander is expected to know how to use his resources to execute the mission at the lowest possible cost, in a way that fits into what the rest of the regiment is doing. It is sometimes an exquisitely complicated business.

Sometime before the plan is all cleaned up and polished, the battalion commander will issue a FRAGO, a fragmentary order that gives the subordinate units some clues about what they can expect and when because they have planning to do themselves. The general rule of thumb for such things is: you get one third of the time remaining from the receipt of the mission to do your planning, your subordinates get two thirds to do theirs.

If you're a company commander you'll be told to arrive at the Combat Operation Center at a certain time—0300 seems to be popular. You'll take your map case, note book, and your key subordinates along. You'll want your weapons platoon commander, artillery forward observer, and the leaders of any attached units to come along. You will bring your messenger and radio operator along, too, with the radio.

The mission you receive will be a variation of the one your battalion commander received, but tailored to the specific mission that the battalion has been given. He refined and adjusted the plan for the battalion—now it is

Lt Col Robert E. (Bob) Lee—no relation—commands 3rd Battalion, 7th Marines, Regimental Combat Team Seven, Fleet Marine Force.

your turn to do the same for your company. You will then issue your order to your platoon commanders who will then do the same. At each step in the process the plan gets simplified, more specific, and more personal. But it still uses the five paragraph format: situation, mission, execution, support, command, and signal.

Keeping an eye on the clock, you develop an estimate and a preliminary plan; then make arrangements for getting the unit to the place where the operation will kick off (the "line of departure"). Advise your subordinate leaders when the op order will be given. Then go out and take a look at the ground, if you can, at the map otherwise—a reconnaissance. After looking at the terrain, you conspire with the other key players, listen to their concerns and recommendations, then decide on the plan and write the op order. Your operations NCO and his helpers will prepare the map overlays and the graphics for the "orders brief."

The platoon commanders will show up—early if they can—and copy the graphics onto their own maps.

Then you issue your order and the platoon commanders take it back to the platoons.

By the time the order gets down to the platoons, the process gets very specific and personal. The whole platoon will probably receive the order together, probably over a "sand table" map of the objective area. The platoon commander will orient everybody, ensuring that there is no confusion about where the objective, supporting units, or the line of departure are. By the time the order gets down to the squads and fire teams in the platoon it sounds something like this:

"*Situation*: an estimated twelve to fifteen enemy with automatic weapons are dug in on Objective 1. I estimate another four to six are dug in on Objective A. A minefield extends across Route 1 into the woods as shown on the map.

"Company D attacks to seize Objective 1 and 2; on order, Company D continues the attack to seize the battalion objective. Company C is on our left.

"3rd Platoon attacks on our right, clears its zone to Phase Line Green, and—on order—continues the attack to seize Objective 2.

"Eight Harriers on ten-minute strip alert are available for support.

"Artillery and the battalion's 81mm mortars are available for support.

"Also, we've got the weapons platoon's machine guns and 60mm mortars for general support.

"*Mission*: Our platoon attacks at 1250 on a frontage of 300 meters; seizes Objective Alpha; on my order, continues to seize Objective 1. Be prepared to continue the attack on order.

"*Execution*: We will attack initially with one rifle squad to envelop Alpha from the right. After the rest of the platoon moves up, we'll take Objective 1 by frontal assault with two squads.

"For the initial attack on Alpha, two rifle squads will provide a base of fire and the assault squad is in general support. Then, when we attack Objective 1, one of the squads and the assault squad will provide the base of fire. Our machine guns will support from the LD.

"Artillery and mortar fires are planned on Objective 1 as follows: AB105 at grid 878729 and AB106 at grid 877728.

"We'll use the Harriers and 60mm mortars on targets of opportunity as the attack develops."

Each of the squad leaders gets detailed instructions for its role in the show, and the platoon leader explains how he wants things coordinated. Finally, he says:

"Everybody carry two frag grenades and a basic load for personal weapons. Ammunition resupply will be after we seize Objective 1.

"If anybody gets hit, the corpsmen will be with 1st and 2nd Squads. The battalion aid station will be 700 meters to the rear on Route 1.

"Prisoners will be handled by SOP.

"Command and signal: the signal to begin the assault and to lift the fires on our Objective Alpha will be red smoke. For Objective 1, it will be red star cluster. I'll use hand and arm signals to displace the base of fires.

"I'll be with 2nd Squad during the attack on Alpha.

"Questions? Okay, it's now 1230. Move out!"

At the very end of the chain of command is the president; he is the ultimate commander, and all combat operations proceed only with

Command of the battle is an art, a science, a ritual older than history.

his approval, followed by the Secretary of Defense, Chairman of the Joint Chiefs of Staff, the Commandant of the Marine Corps. Ultimately, the mission will be assigned to one (or maybe both) of the Fleet Marine Forces.

The FMFs have "building block" components that they use for such purposes. These air-ground task forces have standard formats

Regimental Landing Team Seven Col "Buck" Bedard pops into a combat operations center (forward) to see if everybody's awake.

and are designed for small, medium, and economy-sized emergencies. Each is called a Marine Air-Ground Task Force but Marines usually refer to them in conversation with the acronym "MAGTF" (pronounced "magtaff."). Each is designed to be self-sufficient, mobile, and able to conduct combat operations ashore; each is appropriate for a particular level of threat. And—the great virtue of the system— all are designed to be extremely flexible and adaptable. A commander can take any of these three "plain vanilla" MAGTFs and then add or subtract as appropriate for the particular mission.

The smallest MAGTF is the Marine Expeditionary Unit, called the MEU (and pronounced "mew"). It includes a Battalion Landing Team (BLT) for its ground combat element, a composite squadron for the ACE (airplanes and helicopters), and a combat service support group. There are typically about 2,300 Marines and about one hundred sailors in a MEU. The ACE has thirty aircraft, mostly helicopters, for lift and close air support. The GCE has five tanks and about twenty-five other armored vehicles, a couple of batteries (four tubes each) of heavy and medium artillery, plus mortars, and a heavy battalion of infantry. The commander of a MEU is normally a colonel; he has a planning staff, a communications unit, and a recon and intelligence unit.

There is always a MEU floating around somewhere in the Pacific and another in the Atlantic, waiting for some petty dictator to get indigestion. And when things start to perk on far distant shores that MEU is probably going to be cruising in the direction of trouble. Normally the MEU doesn't have to land to make a point—just having a US Navy/Marine task force arrive offshore is frequently all it takes to have people start minding their manners.

A Marine Expeditionary Brigade is built around a regimental landing team, to produce a substantial combat organization roughly the size of a heavy Army division, with a large slice of the Air Force attached. There are about 15,500 Marines in a MEB, and about another thousand sailors for moral support (including many corpsmen, chaplains, and naval gunfire support teams).

The MEB gets about two dozen F/A-18 Hornets to keep the skies clean of enemy air, about twenty Harriers to pound the enemy on the ground, Cobras to put holes in his tanks and CH-53s, CH-46s, and UH-1s to provide battlefield taxi service and to serve as a kind of military Federal Express, delivering anything and everything to anybody anywhere.

A typical MPS-based MEB will have about fifty tanks, 110 armored assault vehicles, and lots of artillery—including about two dozen 155mm howitzers. It will also get a huge slice of combat engineer equipment, water purification gear, plus all the other things that a Marine needs to conduct business ashore in a hostile clime. This equipment comes right off the ships rather than having to be shipped from the States, and will probably be on-scene before the "main-body" of the MEB arrives.

This "brigade" is custom designed for the particular mission—extra tanks and anti-armor systems for a scenario like Kuwait, less armor and more infantry for a scenario like Grenada or Panama. The beauty of the MPS system is that the ships can carry more than the MEB needs—that they come loaded for alternative problems—will it be jungle or

Projecting power ashore, AAV-style. These big vehicles can carry twenty-five Marines ashore, across the beach, and inland. They are noisy, smelly, and *cramped—but as Marines like to say, the worst ride is better than the best walk.*

desert/urban terrain or rural/cold or hot? The task-organized MEB and the pre-positioned equipment and supplies give the commander some choices that—in the past—he just didn't get.

The Marine Expeditionary Force is a major wartime formation, and in the Gulf war that meant that I MEF was just about the whole active duty Marine Corps. A MEF is task organized for the problem at hand, just like any other, but by the time you've got a MEF you're working with a *big* problem.

A MEF will typically contain the assets of at least one Marine division, an entire Marine Air Wing, and a huge Force Service Support Group to keep it fueled and fed. That means about 45,000 Marines and another 2,600 sailors, about the equivalent of an Army corps. The MEF will have over a hundred fighter aircraft, over a hundred helicopters, plus lots of

One nice thing about Saudi Arabia—the whole place is one big sand table. The lieutenant and his compatriots are building a little model of an objective and will shortly conduct one kind of rehearsal, a sand table exercise. USMC

supporting aircraft. It gets lots of armor, artillery, infantry, engineer, recon, intelligence, and logistics support.

You don't throw a MEF together overnight, and the president doesn't call up and ask for one to get delivered somewhere tomorrow. This is a large, unwieldy, expensive organization and it takes time to put one together. In the Gulf war, I MEF was built up gradually over eight months and ultimately included two Marine Divisions (1st Marine Division and 2nd Marine Division) and most of the active duty Corps, plus many Reservists, about 100,000 Marines in all.

Command Staff

The commander's job may be a lonely one at times, but most of the time he or she gets a lot of company. There is a large staff of officers and enlisted Marines who assemble information, distill it into summaries, prepare orders and maps, all in support of the commander. The commander supervises, provides guidance, and makes decisions on options that the staff assemble, but most avoid micro-management.

A lieutenant colonel will command a battalion. Typically he's been a Marine for about twenty years. He might have done a hitch or two as an enlisted man—many have, and it's excellent preparation for commanding Marines. He'll have played most of the roles in the battalion, and made most of the mistakes. He's been to the Advanced Course, and has spent a lot of his career on "pumps" in the Pacific or the Med. He's probably got gray hair, and he'll have earned it. He knows what a battalion is supposed to do and how a battalion can fail. He'll know a lot of the thousand or so Marines in his unit by name; they will all certainly know his.

The power behind the throne is the Executive Officer, known universally as XO. That doesn't mean hugs and kisses. The XO can usually be recognized as the major with the frantic expression who is attempting to resolve a long list of crises. The XO handles a lot of the administration of the battalion, insulating the commander from the petty detail, letting him deal with the big picture. He is the chief of staff at the battalion level.

Then there is the staff: the S-1 Admin Officer, the S-2 Intel Officer, the S-3 Plans & Ops Officer, the S-4 Supply officer. The XO and the "Three" will usually be majors, the other staff officers normally captains. All are important, but there is a traditional hierarchy that makes the "Three" a very crucial player.

The "Three" is likely to be the "high-speed, low-drag" officer destined for great things. He and his Ops Chief put the operations together, manage the details once the commander decides what he wants to do. They also help the commander with the decision since it is they who prepare the materials he uses to study the options. This section designs and plans the training schedule, in and out of the field. The "Three Shop" is considered the most important of the four by everybody except the Marines in the other three.

The "Four"—who has to do the shopping for the battalion, has to make sure the ammo and the barrier material is on hand for the big attack, and who needs to find 10,000 gallons of fuel when there isn't any to be had—often looks like he's about to pop.

All of these sections are supposed to work together, under the direction of the commander—who is accountable for what they do and fail to do. Afloat, the Navy provides space aboard ship for the Marine commander and his staff to plot and scheme. On a LSD like the *Germantown*, an elaborate center is built into the vessel; its called the TACLOG (for tactical and logistics center), where the various elements of the assault are coordinated before they are established ashore. Of the four functions, perhaps the most critical is that done by the Three Shop, who must design the details of the assault, drawing on the support of the other three sections, integrating everything into a coherent whole. As the assault force moves in on its objective, the planning staff is playing "beat the clock" in a large way. There is never enough time, enough information, enough combat power to guarantee success in the kind of "real world" events that require

Inside the COC (Combat Operations Center). Major Chase is currently master of ceremonies, assisted by the fire-support coordinator, Captain Kinney, and a cast of supporting players. Magnetic markers show the positions of friendly and enemy positions, and are moved as the battle progresses. This team supports and coordinates the efforts of the armor platoon, infantry and engineer companies, artillery batteries, and combat aviation by feeding information, resolving conflicts, and managing time, people, and resources.

Marine intervention. Even though the commander and his staff have a reputation for a lower stress level (hence the derogatory descriptions "staff puke" or "headquarters weenie") and for generating orders and advisories that seem based on fantasy, these poor officers and NCOs probably work as hard as anybody. They have the nasty responsibility to make sure that something useful gets done with all that combat power.

There are two *really* important people in the battalion: one the commander and the other the first sergeant. The commander's primary job is to make the tactical plans; the first sergeant's primary job is to make sure the orders are carried out.

Although the officers typically get the glory, the senior sergeants are normally the people who make a unit a success or failure. The senior sergeant in a battalion or regiment is a Regimental or Battalion Sergeant Major whose job it is to look after the welfare of the enlisted Marines. Officers are required to keep a distance from the enlisted Marines they command; sergeants are not. If a Marine is having marriage or financial problems it is very unlikely that he would turn to his commander for advice, but he will often gladly talk to his first sergeant. When one of these sergeants enters a room it is not unusual for junior enlisted Marines to rise from their seats out of respect, stand at attention, and address him (or sometimes, her) formally.

Other NCOs will attend to the details of the plans and operations orders, for the supplies and schedules, for the intelligence summaries and reports, all helping make the decisions for which the commander takes credit and responsibility. The commander delegates authority and assumes responsibility for the actions of every single Marine in his unit.

A Marine Mission

While still over the horizon, the assault is prepared and launched. Normally, it will begin with a reconnaissance of the defenses by Marines from the recon units. They may swim ashore or be landed in small boats, then will prowl around, making notes and photographs of the beach and its defenses. The recon elements may stay ashore rather than go back to the task force, in which case they transmit their information by satellite radios with scrambler circuits.

Offshore, over the horizon, the planning staff aboard the ships is designing the operation. As information trickles in from the recon teams, satellite photographs and other intel reports, the planners and the commanders develop their plan. Beaches are selected, units assigned to those beaches. Since there isn't enough AAVs and helicopters to take the whole force ashore in a single lift, the assault will be broken down into waves. Planning and communication at this point become critical because individual units will have specific missions to perform during the assault and it is essential that everybody goes ashore on the right beach at the right time. The orders trickle down the chain of command to the platoons and squads who do their own planning and preparation.

Timing becomes critical. The preparation phase begins according to a precise schedule, with naval gunfire and aircraft attacking the beach defenses. While this preparation is being done, the landing force is launched and under way. The Marines come ashore in helicopters or AAVs—usually both. Huge LCACs bring in the heavy equipment like tanks and

LAVs at 50 miles per hour, above the waves. The artillery and air prep should lift just before the assault elements come ashore; if done correctly the defenders will be in a state of shock and unable to react effectively to the assault elements while they are at their most vulnerable.

The first elements ashore typically are charged with securing the beach. Any remaining resistance is reduced and defenses against a possible counterattack are put into position. Then objectives inland are attacked. Usually, this will be done by LAVs or helicopters for speed and battlefield agility. The assaulting

Things get hectic in the COC when you've got artillery shooting, infantry moving, tanks maneuver- *ing, and the regimental commander coming by for a social call.*

infantry will have Harriers, Hornets, and Cobras overhead, on call for close air support. At the same time, other Harriers and Hornets will be conducting deep air support farther inland, attacking enemy units and facilities that might threaten the landing force.

According to the plan, all units have objectives and roles to play. As the assault unfolds, the plan will be modified. But, over hours and days, the objectives are taken and the operation moves toward its goals. Ultimately they are achieved and, on order, the force is withdrawn back onto its ships and the operation is concluded. While this may seem straightforward it is actually one of the most difficult, challenging, and dangerous military operations a combined-arms force can attempt. It is fraught with peril, from both the enemy and from internal problems of communication and coordination. To keep the hazard to a minimum, and based on the experience of amphibious operations in World War II and Korea, the amphibious assault has been developed to a kind of art form.

USS Germantown's *huge well deck accommodates four big LCACs.*

As H-hour approaches for the amphibious task force, vehicle placement on the LCACs is adjusted. Each is securely chained down for the ride across the wave tops.

Assault ships like the Belleau Wood *host all kinds of Marine vehicles, helicopters, and people. To the sailors, all are a bit odd.*

Combat Operations Center Forward. Actual command is shifted from two COCs, the main and the forward. While one manages the battle, the other moves forward to a suitable position and sets up shop and waits for the hand-off. The XO (executive officer) and the Three (intelligence officer) each manage one of the COCs while Lieutenant Colonel Lee tries to keep eyes on the battle and plans for what happens next.

Chapter 4

The Ground Combat Element

There may be four moving parts to a Marine Air-Ground Task Force, but three of them revolve around the ground combat element (GCE), providing support for that young Marine rifleman charging up the beach. The amphibious assault, and the squads and fire teams that execute it, is the very essence of the Corps. Of all the aspects of the mission, this one is the least changed, the one Lieutenant O'Bannon and his Marines at Derna would most easily recognize. After all these years, it still involves coming ashore in small boats with rifles and edged weapons, then closing with an enemy to kill or capture him in personal combat. In many ways, this part of the Marine mission is exactly as it was in 1805. It was then and is now the way combat power is ultimately projected most forcefully and finally when push comes to shove.

The GCE is composed of infantry, armor, artillery, and logistics elements. The planning process will take bits and pieces of the normal regiments and battalions and mix and match them into task forces for specific missions ashore. A platoon of tanks will get "chopped" to an infantry company, an infantry platoon

Squad assault. The left fire team moves while the right suppresses the defenders with well-aimed, sustained fire. These Marines are firing regular ammunition, not blanks, and the hazards are substantial. But if you don't learn to use live ammunition safely in training you'll probably kill or maim your fellow Marines in a combat situation.

The M1A1 Abrams main battle tank is extremely fast, agile, complicated, and expensive. After many years of doubts about its ability to perform on the battlefield, the Abrams confounded its skeptics in Operation Desert Storm by blowing the doors off its competition. Its main gun uses a smooth-bore barrel, along with extremely accurate sensors and an elaborate fire control system, to kill enemy vehicles two miles away with the first shot, day or night, within seconds of their discovery on the battlefield.

might get attached to a company of tanks—it depends on the problem.

Although Marines own tanks, the armor component of a GCE isn't likely to be capable of big tank battles. Instead, tanks are used more to support and protect infantry and the light armor that normally provides the "battlefield taxi" service.

LCAC

Going ashore on an LCAC is an exciting business. It happens at night, probably around midnight. The LSD will probably only come in to about twenty-five miles off the coast for true over-the-horizon assaults. The ship will carry a lot of Marine vehicles and it takes many trips for the LCACs to deliver them all to the beach. The assault force will be briefed hours before the attack is launched. As the time trickles away, the tension rises, and the young Marines joke and chat with increasing animation and laughter. There are final checks of engines, weapons, personnel. A couple of hours before H-hour, the Marines will start stashing rucks and rifles in the LAVs and Humvees. The vehicles for the first assault wave are driven on to the LCACs and chained down early.

Finally, it's time to mount up. Suddenly, despite the hours of standing around, a multitude of small essential chores are discovered, and Marines hustle around, making last-minute adjustments. The drivers and crewmen that will go in on the first wave are nervous. Everybody finds their vehicle and climbs aboard. The ramps come up while Navy LCAC crewmen check the chains and the security of the vehicles. Occasionally a tank or LAV will loosen a chain and thrash around a bit to the distress of all concerned.

The Landing Craft Air Cushion (LCAC) is owned by the US Navy but operated for the Marines. It uses four big aircraft jet turbine engines to "fly" over the waves. Seventeen LCACs supported Operation Desert Storm, operating twenty-four hours straight bringing people, weapons, and vehicles ashore to the 5th Marine Expeditionary Brigade in Northern Saudi Arabia. The LCAC can move at better than fifty knots, with a range of better than 300 miles that lets it operate from beyond the horizon, carrying up to seventy-five tons of M1A1 tanks, trucks, LAVs. It is crewed by five Navy personnel.

The engines start; they are very loud, which is natural because they are large aircraft engines. Both engines drive huge variable-pitch propellers. Control of the craft is done from a cab on the right side forward by a crew of three. The LSDs ramp drops, exposing the well deck to the sea. The LCAC craft master inflates the skirt and the whole huge vessel suddenly rises about five feet on a cushion of air—then starts to slide aft, out of the ship and onto the water. In the LAVs and vehicles the Marines watch and enjoy the moment because there is nothing else to do.

Out of the well deck, the LCAC is surrounded by spray kicked up by its propellers. After a few quick tests the Navy craftmaster decides his odd vessel is airworthy or seaworthy or both, and advances the pitch control. The LCAC floats above most of the waves but nods a bit in response to the swells. Speed increases twenty knots, then thirty, forty, and fifty.

AAV

When it is time for the assault elements to go ashore, most will ride in the modern version of the World War II armored landing craft, today's Armored Assault Vehicle, the AAV. For the individual Marines, it begins about three in the morning with breakfast; then weapons are issued.

"There are hours of preparation before you finally get down to the tank deck," an officer says. I generally stage my platoon on the helicopter deck. The ship is running into the coast in total darkness. You've got to count heads, make sure everybody's present, ready to go." Then the squad and platoon leaders herd their flocks down to the tank deck. Everybody mounts up and settles into the "tracks" and then sits there for about three hours. The platoon leader will command one of the tracks, the platoon sergeant another. It is an anxious time for everybody, but for different reasons. For the platoon leader trying to manage his attachments—the extra people who will help with the platoon mission—there is the difficulty of deciding where to stow the surprise guests. Once everybody gets to the tank deck the leaders do another head count, usually coming up with a different total than the first time. And they count again when the Marines get stowed in the AAVs.

The engines are started and then everybody just sits—for forty-five minutes to three hours. This is generally not considered one of the highlights of a "float," but it can be memorable. Sometimes, out around Japan, the ships can rock and roll about forty-five degrees. Finally, it's show time and the ramp drops from the back of the ship. The AAVs are lined up like ducks in a row. Launch lights burn red, telling the track commanders to stand fast. "It's really great when you're the first off the boat," one platoon leader says. "You're all pumped up, there's all this activity around you, and then the ramp comes down. They give you the warning and all the hatches are secured. I'm in my little commander's cubicle and can see all this! The green light comes on and we just drive right off the ship, into the water. We go completely under water, then come up again. It's wonderful."

One ship can launch a company's AAVs—thirteen or fourteen. They roll off the back, in line parallel to the shore. Then, on command, they all turn toward the shore together and move as a skirmish line. The hatches come open and the commanders and drivers scan the shore line. The .50-caliber machine guns traverse back and forth, searching for targets. Platoon leaders try to establish communications with their other AAVs to make sure that they are all in formation and that there aren't any mechanical problems. At 200 meters off shore, just outside the surf zone, the hatches are buttoned up again for the run into the beach. Depending on the mission, the AAVs may disembark the Marines right there and go back for another load, in which case the track driver will try to find a sea wall or other cover from defensive fires before kicking out the infantry.

"You always have to plan on one of your tracks not making it ashore," the platoon leader says. "It happened to me in exercises, with mechanical problems, and you should anticipate that in combat one of the three will get hit or will broach and not make it ashore. So everybody has to have three sets of plans, and you have to have your assets split up so that you can complete your mission with what makes it ashore."

The AAV-7 is the basic Marine battle taxi. It is a big tracked vehicle that only the very unsophisticated call a "tank." It has tracks similar to tanks, and it may be about the same size, but tanks have armor and AAVs have thin aluminum plate that won't shed projectiles much heavier than a rifle bullet. Just the same, the AAV will take you to the beach in style and a lot more comfort than the Marines who went ashore on Iwo Jima or Peleliu got. You get a little overhead protection from artillery air burst fragments—they got none. The AAV will drive you right up on the beach and over the sea wall, even if the enemy's pinging small arms fire off its delicate hide. Then you can get out and walk around on your own.

The plain vanilla version is twenty-six–feet long and seems big as a house, until

The AAV was originally designed primarily for use in the water, with land operations quite secondary. In practice, though, it has been the other way around. The "antenna farm" on one identifies it as a command track; if you want to make trouble for a Marine unit in combat, shoot at this one first.

you get in. The book says that there's room for twenty-five combat equipped Marines in there, but it doesn't suggest where. It feels crowded with a squad of thirteen aboard if they've brought along the usual accessories: radios, explosives, extra water, and the other necessities of life in the field. On the other hand, Korean Marines are more economical to transport; one Marine officer reports seeing sixty-nine pop out of two AAVs on an exercise.

It is a tremendously versatile piece of equipment that can carry its cargo of Marines from several miles off shore, through seas of up to ten feet, over the beach and deep inland. Not only that, the passengers can get quite a ride. Coming off the ship the vehicle goes com-

pletely under water, sometimes to a depth of eight or ten feet before popping back to the surface.

SRIG

The MEF has a very special little resource, the Surveillance, Reconnaissance, Intelligence Group, commonly called the "SRIG." These Marines set up the outposts, the sniper hides, conduct electronic warfare, maintain the Air/Naval Gunfire Liaison company (ANGLICO), and execute deception operations. It is, in other words, a spooky place. The little band of Marines that got caught in Khafji during the Iraqi attack were a SRIG team—and that probably had something to do with the skill

An AAV is recovered from the briny deep.

The driver's position of an AAV.

Maj Bob Chase is 3/7's operations officer and directs current combat operations while the commander prepares for the battles to come.

and efficiency of their "call for fire." The SRIG owns the radio-controlled airplanes in the division, the Remotely Piloted Vehicles (RPVs) that were developed by the Israelis.

The battalion commander gets a smaller version, the Surveillance and Target Acquisition (STA) platoon, that does some of the same functions. The intelligence officer supervises this platoon.

Snipers

The sniper mission is one of those that seems to come and go out of fashion, sometimes emphasized and sometimes neglected. The Marine Corps has emphasized it more than the Army, and at times it has been something of a minor religion in an institution that considers marksmanship and the rifleman its foundation. Perhaps the greatest American sniper of recent history was Carlos Hathcock, who served in Vietnam and was extremely adept at putting bullets in enemy soldiers at ranges of a kilometer or so, and who bagged over a hundred of them during the war through a combination of talents for marksmanship, fieldcraft, and aggressive tactics.

Now, almost anybody can hit a man-sized target at a kilometer, given a little time, an accurate rifle, and a box of ammunition. Sniping takes the problem to its ultimate, Zen-like extreme. Snipers need to make the first shot hit because there usually isn't an opportunity for another. To do that they have several problems. One is that they have to be able to get in range—something that has nothing to do with marksmanship and everything to do with what is called "fieldcraft." A real sniper must be able to move into position without being seen, sometimes across open terrain in broad daylight, and that can mean crawling hundreds of meters, pulling a bag full of rifle and other tools of the trade.

The Marine Corps sniper has a job that has nothing to do with shooting, too. He is properly called a "scout-sniper," and that means that he may merely observe and report what he sees. This might involve a crawl of half a mile, over the course of half a day or night. Then, without being noticed, they have to build a nest that is so well camouflaged that somebody can literally step on it without noticing them.

In Desert Storm, snipers were used to set up and man outposts to keep an eye on the opposition. This involved putting a team out in a hide, which in this case was a hole in the sand, and keeping them there for days at a time, and keeping them invisible. It is a difficult role, a job with extremely high standards. There isn't somebody always there to tell them what to do and when to do it. Judgment and discipline are as important as—maybe more so—than shooting skills. That's because it takes a lot of mature judgment to know when to shoot and when not to; there's nothing that will stir up the opposing team like having a few of them suddenly start bleeding and thrashing around. Then everybody starts looking for the source of the difficulty with energy and interest. Discovery will result in a rapid cessation of the sniper's ability to keep the commander informed of the activities of the enemy force. So snipers learn to live with missed opportunities.

But when the time comes to fire the weapon, the sniper uses his special rifle with a precision of a brain surgeon. In fact, the sniper is supposed to *be* a brain surgeon of sorts, although the job involves taking it apart without putting it back together. Using the huge .50-caliber Iver Johnson single-shot rifle, a sniper should be able to put his first shot into the head of an enemy tank commander standing (foolishly, as they usually do) in his hatch at a range of about a half a mile. When the commander falls into the turret there will be confusion and dismay that should permit the sniper to perhaps take off the antennas from the tank before the other vehicles in the column know what happened. Leaderless, the enemy becomes vulnerable to anti-armor weapons or friendly tanks. The .50-caliber rifle is stunningly accurate to tremendous ranges, but it only fits certain circumstances. The bolt has to be removed to load each round, so the rate of fire is about as slow as an individual weapon gets. That's why the sniper goes out as part of a two-man pair, and the assistant

brings along an M16 as a portable life insurance policy.

In Vietnam, at the besieged little fortress at Khe Sahn and elsewhere, Marines learned to use the big .50-caliber M2 machine gun—normally an area weapon—against point targets at extreme ranges. For a time, North Vietnamese Army (NVA) troops would expose themselves occasionally, climbing out of their holes a kilometer or so from the wire where they could be seen but not easily shot. It was a way of mocking the Marines in the bunkers,

The tradition is as old as the military: hurry up and wait. They did the hurry-up part earlier and have now been waiting for an hour and a half. When the helicopters show up, they'll hurry again.

and although the enemy soldiers certainly got shot at, they didn't get hit very often. Well, not until scopes were attached to the big M2. The gun is capable of superb accuracy when fired in single-shot mode. The heavy bullet is far less sensitive to little gusts of wind and will hit accurately to long ranges. And those bold, brave soldiers of liberation started getting whacked whenever they were reckless enough to stand up and stretch, taking a lot of the fun out of mocking the Marines.

Sweet Sixteen—the M16A2 Rifle

The ultimate weapon of the entire Corps isn't very sophisticated, is certainly not highly technical, and isn't much different than the old "A-model" version used two hundred years ago. That weapon is the rifleman—a Marine with an accurate weapon and the discipline and good judgment to use it effectively. Although it didn't do a lot of killing in Saudi, that probably had more to do with the amazing good fortune of the task force, rather than anything to do with the rifle's basic validity.

The Marine Corps' emphasis on marksmanship and the value of the rifle goes back only to about the turn of the century, but has become something of a cult since. The M16A2 is an effective weapon only against people, and only to about half a mile. But despite its limi-

A platoon leader offers some friendly advice and en-couragement to his subordinates during a live-fire exercise.

tations, the rifle has won battles for the Corps and every Marine, from commandant to raw recruit, who is expected to be, along with any other skill or specialty, able to fight with the rifle.

When the M16 was developed in the 1950s, it was about as radical a military weapon as anybody could have asked for. At the time, the M1 Garand was still the issue rifle for the Army; it used a clip of eight big .30-caliber cartridges, the same round that fed the World War I Springfield. The AR-15 (as it was originally called) was initially bought by the Air Force who didn't particularly care that its little 5.62mm (.223-caliber) bullet wasn't exactly traditional.

The new weapon was vastly different than the old Garand: plastic stock instead of wood, tiny high-velocity bullet instead of a big, heavy one, only 5.5 pounds empty instead of nine. Despite everything, the Army adopted the rifle after a brief flirtation with the M14. The Marine Corps resisted as long as possible and used the M14 during most of the Vietnam War, but ultimately was defeated by the forces of "jointness." The old advocates of traditional

Lt Col Bob Lee's major problem in these training battles is to keep everybody coordinated and functioning as a team, particularly when things go too fast or slow, things break or fail to show up. Much of the business of command is done before the battle, in training and in planning.

Staff Sergeant Courtney is one of the two AAV commanders assigned to the "3-shop."

Sgt Richard Ita is a member of a recon platoon and has one of the skills that has become part of the Special Operations bag of tricks. He's a scout/sniper, trained to disappear into the woodwork, to watch the enemy, or to engage by fire—either directly or by calling in artillery or airstrikes. The sniper has an important job even if he never fires a shot from that extremely accurate Remington 7.62mm bolt action rifle; he can maneuver across a battlefield unseen, set up a "hide" that is invisible to someone standing on it, and he can report on enemy activity and disposition. And, if he does put the rifle to work, he's capable of killing enemy commanders standing in their tank turrets a kilometer away.

weapons have now mostly died off or retired, and the new Marines accept the weapon and do well with it. Someday the M16 will be the old relic, the traditional weapon of legend and lore, but today it is the very foundation of the Marine Corps.

It weighs about eight pounds with a full thirty-round magazine. You can fire those thirty rounds one at a time or in three-round bursts. If you've learned how to use it you can kill an enemy soldier at up to 800 meters with it, although about 500 meters (about one quar-

ter mile) is a more likely limit. It won't kill a tank, but it will kill the tank commander standing in his hatch—if you're both good and lucky. It will certainly kill the enemy infantry that maneuver with a tank and protect it from people like yourself. When the enemy suddenly appears over the ridge (and they do) and there isn't any close air support or on-call artillery in range (and it happens), then you can either surrender, die, or lock, load, and engage with your personal weapon.

It is easier if they're in the open. They will move at you in bounds, part of the group shooting at you and providing support while the other part of the group runs forward from one bit of cover to another. The traditional thing to do at such moments is to be petrified by fear, particularly the first time it happens. If you and your associates panic, the enemy will easily kill you all. But if you instead each take responsibility for a slice of the landscape around you, and place carefully aimed, disciplined fire on the attackers they will begin to fall. The rifle has a two-position rear sight; flip it to the long-range sight, snuggle into your cozy little hole and use the sand bag as a rest, just as you've practiced on the range. Get control of your breathing, watch your sector. One of the enemy squad emerges from cover at about 500 meters. Smoothly align the sights on his center-of-mass; a breeze is moving the tree tops so hold into the wind about a body width and smoothly squeeze the trigger only while the sights are correctly aligned. Sight alignment and trigger pull are critical; don't try to jerk the shot off—you'll pull it off the target. The first round misses. Concentrate on your priority target, on the sight picture, on the trigger pull. The sound of the enemy fire carries across the battlefield—a little cacophony of pops and stutters at this distance. Their fire begins to sweep your position, little puffs of dirt here and there, a cracking in the air as bullets pass overhead. Take a full breath, let half of it out. Align the sights, place them on the center of mass. Correct for wind. Squeeze slowly, only when the sights are aligned. The rifle speaks and the tiny bullet streaks across the battlefield at a speed of about 3,000 feet per second. It strikes the man in the center of his chest; those nearby will hear an odd, hollow "thwoc" as the soldier folds up, his weapon flies away unattended. He thrashes around but doesn't get up. You just killed a man.

Scan your assigned field of fire. There is a series of flashes, some movement of brush, some green tracers visible out there. You can't see them but there must be an automatic weapon and its crew putting down suppressive fire to support the assault. You can engage them by placing the most accurate fire you can on their position. Not every bullet will hit, but if you shoot carefully and keep up your fire the machine gun will quit one way or another. Squeeze each round off only when the sights are aligned. Watch for evidence of impact and correct your sight picture. Keep up a sustained volume of fire until the enemy fire stops or a more important target appears.

At 200 meters one of the enemy races from one bit of cover to another to your immediate front. Align the sights, put them two body widths in front of his chest and squeeze—he goes down, flopping wildly.

The enemy assault peters out, spent. Survivors withdraw as best they can. Some die in the attempt, others succeed.

It is a difficult lesson, one Americans have learned from enemies and taught as well. One little infantry squad can—if it knows its business—hold off platoons, companies, and occasionally (and in this case, incompetent) battalions of adversaries. The key to this success isn't so much the value of the rifle itself, although it is a bit of technology that has certainly transformed the world; instead, it is the combination of a good rifle and a good rifleman.

This tradition is an American one, and it goes back to the Revolution when primitive backwoods riflemen were killing British "redcoats" at ranges that are respectable even today. Back then the rifle was an advanced bit of technology; the smooth bore musket, with an effective range of only fifty meters or so, was the standard infantry weapon. The rifle

was an eighteenth century "force multiplier," a device that made the side that used it more effective, man for man, than otherwise.

Although a single rifleman can make it very expensive for anyone wanting to defeat him, a team of opponents can do it quite efficiently if they are skilled infantry. But a skilled rifleman who is part of a fire team of four, or a squad of thirteen, or a platoon of fifty-three is a very difficult problem indeed. In fact, the infantry fire team is the smallest example of the concept of combined arms, where different kinds of weapons put many kinds of pressure on the enemy. The rifle puts precision fire on point targets; the squad automatic weapon (SAW) provides a general area suppressive fire, the M203 grenade launcher attached to the squad leader's rifle adds a small version of artillery to the squad's resources. Not only do the individual weapons have mutually supporting capabilities, they are each used by a Marine with a specific responsibility—a field of fire that makes each member of the team more efficient and more focused.

It is very rare for a squad to operate by itself. Instead, squads are assembled into platoons, companies, battalions in combat. Each formation gets an assignment, a role to play—providing and receiving support. The key to making it all work, though, is the skill and discipline of that young Marine with an M16A2 and a thirty-round magazine.

Rifle Platoon

The book says a rifle platoon has forty-two members: three squads of thirteen, a platoon leader, a platoon sergeant and a Navy corpsman. But it seldom happens that way because somebody is always "chopped" to another unit and another mission—and the platoon usually has about thirty-six people in it. In combat (training or real world), however, the platoon acquires various wanderers like Dragon gunners, engineers, a mortar team or others "chopped" to the unit. This again is task organization at the tactical level. These people will be attached to your platoon for as long as they are needed, or survive, or until the company commander wants them for something else. If you happen to be the platoon commander such unexpected company is just part of the routine chaos and you need to learn to deal with it. "You need to be the kind of person who can keep your head in an atmosphere of uncertainty," one officer says. "You might get some kind of support for your mission, you might not; you might get some people you want, you might not. You have to learn to deal with what you get and complete the mission."

As part of the Infantry Officer Course, lieutenants have to do every single job in a platoon: to function as a rifleman, machine gunner, grenadier, squad leader, platoon sergeant. They carry the base plate for the mortar, operate the radio, fire all the weapons. In the process they are supposed to understand the limitations and the resources of every element that they will later command.

The Marine Corps has long thought of the rifle, in the hands of skilled and resolute riflemen, as its fundamental weapon. The A2 version of the venerable M16 has proved to be accurate, reliable, and deadly in combat. It is likely to be around well into the twenty-first century.

Artillery

Despite all the emphasis on the Marine rifleman and on the expensive technologies of the Harrier and Hornet, the biggest killer on the battlefield has historically been artillery. The big guns, normally shooting at a distant and invisible target, have done the majority of killing in every major war since 1900. Many infantrymen, in the Gulf, Grenada, Vietnam, Korea, and before, never actually saw an enemy to shoot during their entire combat tour. One of the reasons is that, in some ways, infantry has become partially obsolete—especially on some kinds of battlefields. Armor, aviation, and artillery have all taken over some of the functions of the foot soldier or Marine: patrolling, screening, and recon are now often done from one sort of vehicle or another.

Infantry isn't—despite the pronouncements of occasional prophets—dead yet as a resource and probably never will be, but artillery makes the job of any soldier in the open difficult and dangerous. That's because modern artillery can put the heat on a target with great accuracy at ranges of up to about fifteen miles, can keep the stuff coming continuously for hours or days, and when coordinated with the rest of the combined-arms team can be decisive.

In the little battle of Khafji, a Marine recon team from the 3rd Marines was trapped in the town when the Iraqis from the 5th Mechanized Division came to call. The little band, led by a corporal named Ingraham, hid out, moving from one building to another, sometimes with the enemy poking around downstairs. But the team was skilled in calling in artillery, and managed to contact 1st Battalion, 12th Marine Artillery Regiment. Ingraham began calling in artillery on targets so close that he had to whisper into the handset of the radio to keep from being overheard.

Peeking over the edge of the roof, the corporal saw an armored personnel carrier arrive in the street below. Out piled about twenty enemy infantry preparing to conduct a house-to-house search of the vicinity. Bringing a new definition to the expression "danger close," Ingraham called in rounds on the Armored Personnel Carrier (APC). The first round hit the APC, splitting it into two untidy halves. The enemy infantry nearby were all killed or wounded. The search of the neighborhood was suspended.

Later, Ingraham called 1/12 again, this time for seventeen enemy armored vehicles out in the street. The first volley destroyed all seventeen vehicles. As they burned, many secondary explosions were observed from the loads of ammunition carried by the APCs. Ingraham adjusted the fires as the surviving enemy infantry attempted to beat a hasty retreat, scoring hits on many.

There are a lot of lessons in that little recon team's big adventure, for both infantry and artillery both. One of the lessons is that artillery can put a tremendous crimp in the plans of an infantry or armor task force *if* the artillery has the benefit of a good observer with "eyes on the target," a tactical fire direction center to accurately plan the fire mission, and an accurate gun, skillfully laid. Without that recon team in the town, actually calling in accurate data on the enemy, the accurate gun would have been useless. Infantry can be tremendously vulnerable to such fires, but the Iraqis could have done more to deal with the observers—by thoroughly searching buildings, for one thing. The recon team could have been located with the kind of system American infantry uses, the PRD-11 Emitter Locator System, which pinpoints the source of radio transmissions, but the enemy's attack was essentially incompetent. Against a better enemy, Ingraham and his compadres would have been dead meat.

Marine artillery is an integral part of most missions. Each Marine division has an artillery regiment to supply assets for MAGTFs.

M198 155mm

The weapon of choice for these battalions is the huge M198 howitzer, a 155mm (6-inch) gun that will put steel on target at fifteen miles with conventional ammunition and to nearly nineteen miles with rocket-assisted projectiles. It comes in two versions, both big:

one is towed or lifted by big helicopters, the other is self-propelled—but on the ground only. Both will deliver high explosive rounds of several kinds; white phosphorus for incendiary, antipersonnel, marking, and other purposes; and the Copperhead laser-guided projectile that is extremely accurate. There are also projectiles available in 155mm that will dispense little submunitions that can destroy light armored vehicles, trucks, and people in the open, and Field Artillery Scatterable Munitions (FASCAM) rounds that spread little time-delay bomblets across a wide area.

M101 105mm Howitzer

Another long-time favorite is the good old M101, a 105mm gun that is the direct descendant of grand-dad's old World War II howitzer that he took to Germany with the 2nd Armored Division. It's light (for an artillery piece), which means it goes everywhere that a truck can go. It's handy for artillery raids, and if you happen to be defending a position with one and the enemy starts wading through the wire in the middle of some dark and stormy night, try launching a few "beehive" rounds at them. This projectile works only at short range, but its hundreds of little steel darts spread out when they leave the muzzle and scream across at the enemy with a sound like a trillion angry banshees. It is a bit like firing a shotgun at the assault, and if they are in range—about three hundred meters is about right—all the good intentions and warrior spirit goes right out of the enemy attack. That's because a very large number of them will be, as they say, "in a world of hurt." It is a weapon of last resort, but it worked wonders in Vietnam and it hasn't had to be used often since.

M109 SP

The M109 is a 155mm howitzer with its own set of tracks and a cute little trailer to keep the gun crew supplied with ammunition. It looks like a tank, but the armor is only half-inch aluminum. The M109 is intended to provide mobile heavy artillery to the armor on the move, with all the virtues of the big howitzer and the mobility of a tracked vehicle.

M110 8-inch Howitzer

Marines also use the 8-inch/203mm howitzer on a self-propelled carriage, but there are only twelve of this huge, obsolete gun in the regiment, and all are in the 5th battalion, the place the big self-propelled guns call home. It is too big to go places in a hurry, but it will fire a nuclear warhead when it gets there, if push comes to that much shove.

The Fire Mission

The trick in artillery isn't just hitting the target, it's putting the very first round on target at the moment it is supposed to be there—a very complex problem when the target is on the other side of some distant ridge. There are basically three components to the system: the gun, the fire direction center, and the observer who is actually looking at the target and making what is referred to as "the call for fire."

In order to deliver really accurate first round projectiles, a gun crew needs to know exactly where the target is and exactly where their own gun is. That's traditionally been a problem, but most Marine units and all Marine gun batteries now have little hand held satellite receivers that will tell you where in the world you are, to within a few feet. During Desert Storm maps became essentially useless during much of the ground combat phase be-

A sergeant normally leads a squad of thirteen Marines.

cause of the few terrain features and the inky skies. But the little GPS (for Global Positioning System) receivers could tell a company commander in a fight exactly where he was and by using that position as a reference he could call down the wrath of the supporting artillery on the opposing team.

Observed Fire Procedures

Artillery is a kind of art and science and another one of those little sects within the Corps that attracts a certain kind of individual. For the most part artillerymen are mathematicians. Sending that projectile downrange is a simple task; getting it where and when it is supposed to arrive is a different problem all together. For example, a 155mm gun and crew can execute a time-on-target (TOT) mission that will put three rounds into the air, one after another, and have them all explode on the target at the same instant. That kind of massed fire is really effective in some situations—troops in the open, for example—where three rounds in succession would let the target find a place to hide. To do a TOT mission requires the gun's fire direction center (FDC) to shoot the first round up into space on a high trajectory, the second at a lower and shorter trajectory, and the third on a flat, direct trajectory. Properly done, the rounds all detonate at the same devastating moment. Very impressive, particularly if you're the target.

Despite the size of the gun, the 105mm gun crews train to move into a firing position, set up the gun, receive a fire mission, shoot it, and be on the road again before the rounds hit the target.

Much of the success of Marine artillery is the result of what happens inside the little vehicle that serves as the fire direction center (FDC), normally located well away from the guns. It doesn't look like much from the outside, but the FDC is the brains and heart of the system and the guns are just the muscle. Fire missions are called into the FDC; when one is received, the battery is alerted over the radio with a warning order. "Fire mission!" is how it begins. The gun crews stop eating their MREs and repeat the command, running to

The Shoulder-launched Multi-purpose Assault Weapon (SMAW) is a bunker-busting weapon that can also be used against lightly armored vehicles—but not tanks. The projectile is an 83mm rocket that is good to about 400 meters. The SMAW is owned and usually operated by the support platoon of an infantry company, with six of the systems available to be "chopped" to missions as the commander orders.

their positions. As the firing data is transmitted, they will all repeat the data at the top of their voices, a sort of battlefield Marine chorus. The FDC will tell the battery how much to elevate their tubes, the traverse angle, and the charge—the amount of powder—for the round. The Marine who is responsible for the charge will cut one or more bags of propellant from those inside the cartridge; a "charge six" shot will involve the removal of three of the nine bags in the case. He'll then slide the projectile into the case neck, and another member of the gun team will hold it near the breach until commanded to load. Finally, the FDC calls over the radio: "At my command. . . FIRE!"

Howitzers are comparatively low-velocity weapons with arcing trajectories that may take ten or fifteen seconds before impact. That means that you can stand behind the gun and watch downrange and watch the round depart, a black dot rapidly disappearing into space. The FDC will call the observer about this time and call, "Shot." This alerts the observer to observe the hit and offer corrections.

There are many variations on the theme, with many kinds of fire missions, types of ammunition and fuse, and tactical problems.

The first three battalions are normal assets of the Marine division and available for assignment to a MAGTF as one is assembled. But the fourth battalion of every artillery regiment is dedicated to travel and is always deployed with the MEU on a "float." And the fifth battalion is dedicated to the heavy self-propelled guns, the 8-inch and 155mm SPs.

Forward Observers

Although there are dedicated, professional forward observers whose business it is to make the call for fire, in fact, anybody with a radio and the code words to authenticate his request can do it. The procedures are taught to most Marines so that a patrol leader, an LAV commander, or a scout-sniper can all call down the wrath of the FDC on a target. There is a little ritual to it, a bit like a three-act play. The first act is an identification and warning; the second locates the target; the third describes the target and what is to be done to it. It usually starts with a company commander in trouble or maybe a recon Marine hiding in a hole. On the net he'll call:

"Fire mission."

"Zulu Five Seven, this is Zulu Seven One: Adjust fire, over."

Over his own radio he'll hear the FDC call back, "Zulu Seven One, this is Zulu Five Seven: Adjust fire, out."

"Grid 180513, over."

The FDC acknowledges and reads back the location: "Grid 180513, out."

The big M198 155mm howitzer can loft a shell about twenty-five miles. Artillery has traditionally been the biggest killer on the battlefield.

The observer has spotted an enemy infantry platoon to his front, so he identifies the target for the FDC who need to know what kind of fuse to employ—in this case, an air burst will be desired. "Infantry platoon in the open. ICM in effect, over."

"Infantry platoon in the open. ICM in effect. Authenticate Papa Bravo, over."

"I authenticate Charlie, out."

"Message to Observer Zulu: Two rounds; target AF1027, over."

"Message to Observer Zulu: Two rounds; target AF1027, out."

"Direction 1680, over."

Tanks

The role of armor in Marine operations is quite different than in the Army, where massed armor formations go head-to-head with similar enemy formations. Marines may own and operate the same M1A1 Abrams main battle tank but use it in platoons rather than in battalions. Tanks proved their utility in the amphibious operations in the south Pacific during World War II by saving the day for Marines trapped by Japanese machine gun emplacements and bunker complexes. The Shermans were few in number (and those numbers were rapidly abraded to nearly zero by enemy artillery), but while they survived, the landing force in the vicinity of each was able to move inland. The tank and infantry team provided mutual protection that saved Marine lives and consumed those of the enemy. It was a good combination—and tanks are used today in essentially the same way.

Of course, there is a lot of armor on the battlefield—AAVs and LAVs in profusion—but the lightly armored vehicles need protection too since each is vulnerable to any weapon over .50 caliber, particularly the missiles and rockets that are designed for their thin hides. So along comes the big M1 tank to lead the force through the breech on a dark and stormy night.

Riding in an M1 Abrams tank in the middle of the night is an experience that takes some getting used to. Standing in the loader's hatch on the left side of the turret you can watch the terrain slide past, the tracks adding a rumbling roar that vibrates gently through the hull. The tank is big—twenty-five-feet long—and bulky, but it seems to glide across the terrain, floating. The gun tube has been aimed at a target off to the side; despite twists and turns the tube remains fixed on that target. From the loader's hatch, the sensation is that the hull of the tank moves in an extremely odd way beneath you, but it is only an illusion.

Inside the turret are three crew stations; a fourth, the driver's, is isolated up front in the hull. The tank commander, usually a sergeant or a lieutenant, stands or sits on the right. In front, lower, sits the gunner. His only window on the world is his little televised view that comes through his gun sight. The loader usually stands, his station on the left of the big breech of the 120mm gun.

The loader is usually a strong, quick young Marine who likes to lift weights. That's most of what he does—fifty-five-pound ones, full of propellant and explosives and depleted uranium.

The commander spots a target through the smoke and dust, a T-72 tank moving quickly towards us two kilometers away. Things happen fast inside a tank in combat. You will kill or be killed within about twenty seconds. "Target!" yells the tank commander, his version of a warning order. He takes control of the turret using the commander's override switch on his control and quickly slews the turret to the target, putting the tank in the sight. He and the gunner both see it as a white blob on a black field, like an out of focus video shot by a four year old. The driver is maneuvering hard but the target is locked into the sight, automatically, under computer control.

"Tank!" yells the commander over the intercom. "Sabot!" he yells again, a one word order to the young loader, telling him to load a sabot round.

The loader presses his right knee against the switch, and the ballistic doors that protect the ammunition zip open revealing the racks

The laser designator, operated here by PFC Keith Timken, can mark a target with coded laser light that provides a homing source for missiles like the Hellfire and the Copperhead artillery round fired by the M198 155mm howitzer. This lets the Cobra or the artillery battery launch their round into the general vicinity of the target; the designator can provide the terminal guidance. The systems' range is several kilometers, which keeps the forward-air-control (FAC) team safe and sound when the shooting starts.

of shiny aluminum rounds. The loader has identified the type of each on the base with a felt marker; he pops an armor-piercing, discarding-sabot round out by striking the base and retainer clip with his fist. Then he extracts it, spins the heavy round end-for-end, and rams it into the open breech, which slams shut by itself. "Up!" the loader reports.

"Fire!" yells the commander, and the gunner, who has already entered the ammunition type into the computer, lased the target with a laser range finder, and aligned the sight on the target's center-of-mass, presses the trigger.

There isn't much noise from the gun inside the buttoned-up turret, but the M1 rocks a bit from the recoil. Through the sight the gunner and commander see the bloom of the projectile

gasses, the little glow of the tracer on the back of the dart, then the impact of the round on the enemy tank a mile away. The projectile is only a slender piece of metal, without any explosive in it at all, but it is very, very heavy, and the gun makes it go extremely fast. It is shaped like a dart, and that's the way it flies across the battlefield at nearly a mile a second. The result is enough kinetic energy to melt through the armor of any conventional tank, with dramatic results. If it penetrates, and it probably will, the inside of the hull will be spattered with white-hot chunks of metal. They will probably kill or incapacitate the crew instantly. One way or another, things in the turret will catch fire.

Three basic things happen to a tank when hit by a shot from another. One is that it can gradually catch fire over five or ten seconds before becoming a raging inferno as the propellants and the fuel ignite, "brewing up," the British call it. Another is that the tank can almost instantly come apart in a large explosion if its rounds detonate instead of merely burn. The final thing is that the tank can shed the round and engage you, the adversary, in return.

The Abrams is a fairly new addition to the Marine Corps, a successful transplant from the Army. It is a tremendous improvement over the old faithful M60 that has served for years, but whose gun, armor, and power plant have all become obsolete. Having the same main battle tank as the Army uses has some advantages for the Corps, particularly when it comes to cost.

It seems that all nations claim that their main battle tank is the best anywhere, and the Army and Marines certainly claim that about the Abrams. The Brits say their Challenger is the best, and the Russians probably think their T-80 is the greatest thing on tracks. And all of them might be right, too, depending on how you measure best. One British gunner decided to test his gun system against an Iraqi tank over three miles away—about twice as far as normal engagement range and well beyond the published maximum ranges for any NATO gun system. He fired at the tank and it came unglued from the first round.

The Abrams used by the Marines has a 120mm smoothbore gun that turns out to be wonderfully accurate. Its armor is the new composite type, probably using ceramics and other materials in layers that will protect the crew as well as many inches of traditional steel armor, but with far less weight. It is powered by a Lycoming 1,500-shaft-horsepower gas-turbine engine—a fairly radical innovation, much criticized when it was introduced. The engine consumes fuel at a rapid rate—it will go about 300 miles on a tank of fuel (about 500 gallons). In other words, you get about two-gallons-to-the-mile fuel economy (highway) and a lot worse (city). But since the thing weighs about 25,000 pounds, what did you expect?

The M1 carries aboard forty rounds for the main gun, plus a few hundred rounds for the .50-caliber machine gun and the M60 used by the loader against low-flying airplanes.

Each Marine division includes a tank battalion, and these are configured a bit differently than other Marine battalions because there are four (not three) companies. The tank battalions have a little headquarters element like the other battalions, but they have a recon platoon and an anti-tank company, too. There are about a thousand Marines in a tank battalion, and another twenty sailors providing support.

A standard platoon gets five tanks with one officer and twenty-one enlisted Marines. Big tank battles are supposed to be the business of the Army's tank divisions, but the Marines attacking into Kuwait got into a huge fight in the Al Burquan oil field.

But the way it is supposed to work and the way Marines train, is for the tank battalion to have its companies "chopped" to the infantry battalions and infantry companies "chopped" to the battalions—a process called "cross attachment." The result is yet another task-organized hybrid designed for whatever little excursion the commander and his "staff pukes" have invented. The relationship is hardly more than a brief flirtation—one date and its over. The tanks are particularly welcomed by the infantry, though, because they can avert a lot of the annoyance of dealing with bunkers,

The call for fire. The forward air controller (with map and radio handset) is a Marine pilot temporarily assigned to a ground combat element. His job is to coordinate the close-air-support mission, making sure the bombs and bullets fall on the enemy rather than on the Marines. The FAC normally has the services of a radio operator, a Marine who can also operate the laser-designator and provide security for the team when necessary. Capt Greg Glasser is a CH-46 pilot in real life but is serving a tour with 1st Battalion, 9th Marines as a FAC (forward air controller).

enemy light or heavy armor, or other nuisances of an infantry assault.

Light Armored Infantry

"We're going to try to avoid the road at all costs," the platoon leader says just before the assault. "Instead of driving up the main road—a great place to get your ass shot off—we're going to go around, through the hills where the enemy hopefully won't be expecting us." They'll be taking a platoon of light armored infantry (LAI) in a hook to come at the objective from what they hope will be a lightly defended rear area. And, instead of just blundering up the road into one of what must certainly be an ambush or two, they will move in short bounds. The lead LAI will advance, observe, and prepare to shoot back if anything develops; then the other vehicles in the task force will move up, like a big, mechanized inchworm on the move. The lead vehicle uses the thermal night sight on his TOW (Tube-launched, Optically tracked, Wire guided) system to scan the terrain. Any heat source will show up, even on the darkest, rainiest night, as a white glow against a green and black background.

"We use the 'inchworm' or 'bump' method for covering a danger area when there's not a lot of room to maneuver," the platoon leader says, but out in the desert we can use 'bounding overwatch,' which is a faster way to get across." He studies the map laid out on top of his LAV. The platoon's primary objective is a little spot near the airfield that the Army's paratroopers may or may not manage to seize. If they succeed, the two forces will establish a link-up at the spot on the lieutenant's map. If the Army fails to arrive, the platoon and the other forces in the area—those that survive to

The M1A1 main battle tank is the same one the Army uses, but Marines use it in far smaller numbers and for different tactical applications.

get this far—will have to take the field themselves.

As the hours tick slowly away before the platoon drives onto the LCACs and gets bussed ashore by the Navy there is plenty of time to wonder what will go right and wrong with the plan. Platoon leaders, maybe more than any other Marine, tend to be pessimists. Everything that can go wrong probably will, sooner or later. So the lieutenant considers his options and odds: "If the enemy *is* in this area and if we *can't* link up with the Army we'll have to change the plan. And I just don't see us hightailing it up this road like we're supposed to." The terrain lends itself to good anti-armor tactics. The lieutenant looks at the map and identifies several excellent ambush sites. He spent eight years as an enlisted Marine as an anti-tank team member, so the first thing he does is consider what he would do to defeat the mission he's been given. "If I were on the other side," he says, "and I knew there were only eight vehicles coming at me, I'd take eight gunners with AT-4s or Dragons—and I could do three 'massed surprise fires' and take out all four vehicles!" So the platoon leader avoids that particular set of coordinates and plans his route to include a much safer although more rural drive.

The LAV was designed in Switzerland and is known in Europe as the Mowag Piranha. The design is something quite new for the

The 120mm anti-tank rounds are incredibly accurate to a distance of about a mile, a distance they cover in about a second. The projectile is a slender dart made of depleted-uranium alloy—an extremely *heavy, hard material that uses kinetic energy rather than chemical explosives to punch through enemy armor.*

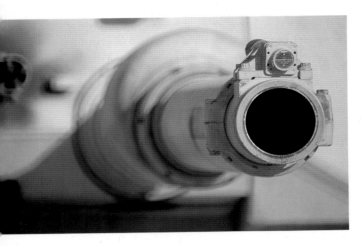

The business end of the 120mm main gun.

The LAV comes in several variants: a plain vanilla version, with the 25mm gun and room for six infantry; a command version for the boss to ride in, with a rack of radios and a couple of people to operate them; a TOW version for the anti-tank mission; plus another variant with the big 81mm mortar taking up most of the back. There's also a recon version, a logistics version, and even a recovery LAV to pull the others out of the mud. All of them have light armor, an aluminum alloy plate that will shed rifle fire and most artillery fragments but not anti-armor rounds or heavier machine gun fire like that from the popular four-barrel, 23mm ZSU-23-4 anti-aircraft battery used by many potential adversaries.

The accommodations vary. The crew is normally three: a driver, a commander, and a gunner. Passenger legroom varies from plenty to negligible, depending on where they put you and what else is aboard. It can get mighty cramped in back, but the radio operators in the command version get nice executive chairs.

LAVs have a battalion all their own. It fields three companies of the plain "battlefield taxi" variant, each with fourteen vehicles plus two command LAVs. The weapons company gets sixteen of the anti-armor version with the TOW missile launcher and eight mortar LAVs. The headquarters company gets the recovery vehicle, two command versions, and the logistics variant for the S-4 shop to deliver groceries.

The American military resisted this kind of vehicle for a long time—and with good reason. The possibility of NATO banging heads with the Warsaw Pact was pretty substantial. The armor on these kinds of vehicles isn't. Armor commanders didn't want to risk having a bunch of thin-skinned, vulnerable vehicles cluttering up the cramped, confined battlefields of northern Europe where they expected to fight the Red Horde's massed divisions of genuine tanks. Even an old T-62, a thirty-year-old design, should have been able to clean the clock of a whole company of LAVs in a war. Reluctantly, the United States accepted

American military, although it's been popular with the rest of NATO for decades: wheels instead of tracks for high speed on roads and eight wheels to spread the weight across the ground better than four, as used with some other light armor. It came into service with the Corps in 1985 and has quickly become an essential part of the Marine ground forces.

Wheels make high speed travel a lot easier on roads than tracks, and the LAV will go a whole lot faster than your company commander wants you to drive. It is officially rated at being able to do 60 miles an hour, max, but unofficial reports give it more credit. "We had this thing up to eighty," one driver says, "and it was just like driving a Cadillac!" The LAV actually is something of a Caddy, but without the leather upholstery, and its stereo system only gets the tactical channels. The driver's position up front has the usual controls in the usual places: steering wheel, brake, and selector levers for the automatic transmission and the transfer case. But you get lots of extras on an LAV that are not available on a Caddy, including a great fire-suppression system and a night sight for those excursions in the dark. Besides that, there's the terrific 25mm chain gun for dealing with any battlefield traffic cops.

the need, though, for light armor to provide follow-on support and cavalry missions for the main armored thrusts. The M-2 Bradley was the solution to the problem—and still is, a great system that is serving the Army well.

But other NATO nations accepted the idea of the lighter, cheaper, more vulnerable wheeled vehicle and developed it to a minor art form. American planners finally accepted the idea too, and the Army is using the Mowag design now along side the Bradley.

The mission for the LAV companies is a kind of cavalry role, although the Marines don't use that expression. But they use the LAV for the traditional cavalry jobs—screening, recon, deep strike, pursuit, harassment. It is a mission that requires speed, agility, and only moderate firepower. Cavalry, from the days of horse and before, has always relied on speed in place of armor and has often been an important element in combat. In contemporary combat LAVs free up tanks from screening and recon missions that don't use their talents well. And they are cheap enough to be prolific, and prolific enough that the infantry can get some industrial strength fire support

that moves along with the assault, going places a tank doesn't belong.

"I think it's going to go fast, real fast," the lieutenant says. "Coordination is going to be tough up in through here but I've got some great NCOs. An hour and a half, max!"

Force Recon

The Army has its Rangers and Green Berets (and, although we aren't supposed to talk about it, the super-select unit called Delta) and the Marines have Force Recon. It is an elite group with a special mission. There are three battalions, one for each division, but they are essentially responsible to the Fleet Marine Forces. That's because they have missions that are fundamental to the big MAGTF missions that the FMFs generate.

Force Recon battalions use the same "triangular" model that the rest of the Corps employs, three companies (and a headquarters) with three platoons each. The platoons have four recon teams with four men in each. They are trained in many of the same skills that Green Berets and others in the special-operations community receive, for the same reasons.

The LAV's big wheels permit high road speeds and cross-country mobility.

Force Recon is designed to spend a lot of time in the backwoods of the enemy, gathering information or wreaking very special kinds of havoc.

Force Recon Marines are just about the few on "jump" status and who get sent to the Army's Basic Airborne School at Fort Benning, Georgia. There the instructors take special delight in tormenting their brothers-in-arms with plenty of extra pushups and similar tests of physical conditioning, just to see who's the toughest of the tough. Marines like tormenting the "black hats" right back by doing the extra pushups and then adding a few in honor

of the Corps, sometimes one handed out of spite. During World War II there was a Marine parachute battalion but it didn't get the glory of the Army's five airborne divisions and was ultimately dispensed with.

If those rough, tough Army paratroop instructors ever tried to go along on Force Recon missions they'd wish they'd been a lot nicer to the Marines because the kinds of skills and hazards are a lot more challenging than stepping out of a perfectly good airplane. Recon Marines can parachute into enemy territory, but the static-line method of insertion is really sissy stuff compared to the HALO (high-alti-

An LAV on the move. The LAV comes in many variants: full of radios, for command and control, with TOW missile launchers for anti-armor engagements, and as a "plain vanilla" battlefield taxi for Marine infantry.

tude exit from the airplane, typically 20,000 feet, low opening of parachute, typically 800 feet) or HAHO (high-altitude exit, high parachute deployment that allows a jumper to glide under his canopy for many silent miles).

That's still sissy stuff compared to some of the insertion techniques that Recon uses, including coming ashore in a rubber boat from a submarine. Rubber boats are notoriously bad at providing protection from bullets, artillery fragments, or almost anything else the enemy might throw at you.

Recon Marines go through a training program that makes boot camp look like a church picnic. Classes are seven weeks long, for carefully selected and tested candidates. Since the mission of Force Recon is pre-assault and post-assault reconnaissance of beaches, roads, bridges, and enemy defenses and facilities, Marines who sign up for the training have to be prepared for a lot of travel. Classes are conducted in helicopter insertion and extraction techniques, patrolling, and use of weapons, scuba equipment, and radios. Each swims about three miles a day; to graduate, they will make the swim at night, wearing full combat equipment.

MREs

After a hard day defending freedom and democracy you'll probably be ready to sit down to a nice, big, hot dinner of maybe steak and potatoes washed down with a tall glass of some sort of carbonated refreshment. Forget it—you're getting an MRE and a canteen cup of warm water. "MRE" officially means "Meal, Ready-to-Eat" but Marines have other, less polite, versions—one of which is Meal, Rejected by Ethiopians.

Feeding people in the field has always been a problem. In the past armies have solved it by stealing what they need from the countryside surrounding the route of march. That has gone out of favor in recent years. Instead, a lot of effort has been put into finding food that could keep for a long time, is compact and light enough to carry, and provides enough calories for a combatant. If the troops

actually liked the stuff, it would be entirely by accident.

During the North Africa campaign of World War II, the British 8th Army managed to defeat Rommel and the Afrikakorps on a diet of canned corned beef, jam, and tea—virtually nothing else for weeks and months on end. American soldiers and Marines were sometimes not much better off; the K-ration of the time came in a little box and contained a vile little protein bar, some ghastly stale crackers, a couple of pieces of gum, and five cigarettes. A bit of toilet paper was included, without much motivation.

An LAV chained down aboard an LCAC, ready to go ashore with the first assault wave at midnight. The LAV is a Swiss design that is lightly armored but able to shed most artillery fragments; it is fast, agile, and able to jump tall hills with a single bound. Its 25mm gun will tear up anything lighter than a tank—especially trucks, bunkers, and infantry dumb enough to expose themselves to its fire.

83

The C-ration came later, with canned ham and lima beans, canned pound cake, canned fruit cocktail, a candy bar that wouldn't melt in your hand or your mouth—and five stale cigarettes. By combining the little packet of coffee creamer with the instant cocoa packet and the sugar Marines in Vietnam discovered that they could tolerate the stuff. Marines tried just about every possible combination of ingredients to add some variety to the menu. Almost everybody had a favorite component and a least-liked entree; one young machine gunner in particular survived on the pound cake and fruit cocktail for days at a time.

Then along came MREs and the great debate. Which was better, "C-rats" or MREs? Well, MREs are much lighter, more compact, and a lot easier to deal with in the field. But the old C-rats had a loyal following among the

Need a lift? The technique is called the Special Purpose Insertion and Extraction System (SPIES) and is handy for those quick getaways when the party's gone sour.

old guard that was used to them, even if they were heavy. The fruit cocktail is now freeze-dried and looks like styrofoam with clots. The candy bar still won't melt. But the entrees come in little pouches that are easy to heat, open, eat from, and dispose of. You can have spiced beef slices, beef stew, or a freeze-dried pork patty that looks like a brown styrofoam hockey puck—until you add water and let it sit a while. The new ones have regular packages of candy in them—real M & Ms sometimes—and tiny bottles of Tobasco sauce for those Marines with indelicate palates. The stale cigarettes, however, are long gone.

Actually, most Marines like MREs the first twenty or thirty times they eat them. Considering the mission of the little brown plastic bags, just about everybody thinks they're a successful solution to the problem of what groceries do you really want to carry with you on the camping trip. Each is supposed to contain about 1,300 calories, although to get that much from one you'd probably have to consume everything, including the plastic bag they come in.

The real problem with them is the monotony. After you've tried the tuna casserole, BBQ beef, ham slices, and the omelet with ham chunks a few times the menu will need to be enlivened. That's when Marines start getting creative and mix the contents into some remarkable nouvelle-cuisine creations, like adding the crackers and cheese spread to the chicken a la king. After a week of such tame inventions, the really brave Marines start experimenting with really creative combinations—like putting the freeze dried coffee, sugar, creamer, Tabasco sauce, fruit mix, peanut butter, M & Ms, and the cocoa mix in with (for example) the meatballs-beef-and-rice-in-tomato-sauce entree; it all goes in a canteen cup and gets heated, sometimes over a little chunk of burning TNT (a great fuel if you don't have a stove). This is usually the clue for the commanders that it is just about time to call "endex" (end of exercise) and go home; when the Marines start adding the "bug juice" beverage powder to the vat and *liking* it, everybody knows its really time to get out of the field.

T-Rats

But, if the Four Shop has done its duty, you will get an occasional hot meal out in the field, perhaps with some fresh fruit and cartons of milk if you've been good. Until fairly recently hot food in the field was a big problem—several problems, really. The first was preparing it, and that meant setting up kitchens, cooking, and cleaning up. Although it took tremendous effort and resources, they did it in World War II and Korea and occasionally in Vietnam. The other problem was disease. It is hard to keep everything sanitary and one of the most memorable things about the process was something called the "GIs."

Then T-rats were invented. These are large, flat tins in which are some amazingly good entrees that can be heated simply by placing them in hot water. The scrambled eggs with bacon are excellent and so is the lasagna; the pork slices don't look or taste like styrofoam but instead resemble good pork roast. The canned vegetables still taste like canned vegetables, but there is a canned crumb cake that makes up for it. And instead of a stainless steel mess kit to accumulate bacteria, they serve you on paper plates and nobody gets sick from the food anymore. True, the house burgundy is called "bug juice" and tastes like Kool-Aid, but compared to warm water from a plastic canteen it is just fine.

Nouvelle cuisine, Marine style. To the standard meatballs in tomato sauce, this Marine has added crackers, cheese spread, and a whole (tiny) bottle of Tabasco sauce. Others have been known to add coffee, M & Ms, and the fruit mix to the entree—and allege to enjoy the combination.

They call it "Ma Duce," but, officially, it is the M2 Heavy Machine Gun, Caliber .50, a weapon that goes back to the 1930s and remains an excellent, accurate, dependable way of killing people and destroying property efficiently and at long ranges.

Chapter 5

Marine Air

The Air Combat Element (ACE) is, by Marine doctrine, one quarter of the concept and one half of the killing component of a task force. This incorporation of aviation and emphasis on its role is one of the things that makes the US Marine Corps special in the world's armed forces. Other services, like the US Army, rely on independent air forces for at least part of their aviation needs—and that often has created problems in the past. But Marines learned early, first in World War II and later in Korea, that "owning" the airplanes made a big difference in the quality of the support you got from them. Now they own a lot of them and use them for a large part of the mission.

The Beginnings of Marine Air

Marine aviation began the way a lot of programs in the Corps seem to, with the personal initiative of one officer. In this case it was Alfred Cunningham, a first lieutenant, who became intrigued with the idea of flight in 1911, about the time the Wright brothers were promoting their invention. Cunningham rented, at his own expense, a machine that was supposed to be capable of flight and spent con-

A vital part of the Marine air mission is the assault-support component—moving infantry quickly to critical objectives across the battlefield. And the CH-53 is a star performer at this task, a huge, powerful, multi-talented airframe.

siderable time attempting to get it airborne, without success. But he at least got himself sent to flight school, and was certified the first Marine aviator in 1912.

Marine aviation didn't get to accomplish many great deeds during World War I—one company, assigned to anti-submarine patrols, never saw a sub during the war. But it was a beginning, and after the war, air power began to be integrated into Marine doctrine.

Close air support was invented by Marines flying old DH-4s left over from World War I during the second expedition to Nicaragua in the 1920s. One of the numerous little battles that Marines fought during the Banana Wars occurred at Ocotal on 15 July 1928, about 0100, when a fire fight developed between rebels and a force of less than a hundred Marines and Nicaraguan guardsmen. Two patrolling DH-4s came by the next morning and figured out what was going on. One started to blast away with the aged aircraft's multi-purpose ring-mounted .30-caliber gun, hosing what the gunner hoped was the enemy positions until all the ammo was used up. Later that afternoon four of the aircraft came back with the early version of today's "pig iron" (as the conventional gravity bombs are called), except that these were 25-pounders instead of the 500-pound models used now. The DH-4s made diving attacks and scored heavily on the opposition. Fifty-six rebels were found afterwards, expired, and another hundred or so were wounded. Marine losses in the escapade were one dead and five wounded.

By 1939, with war clearly in everybody's future, the Navy's general board defined the role for Marine fliers: Marine Aviation is to be equipped, organized, and trained primarily for the support of the Fleet Marine Force in landing operations and in support of troop activities in the field; and secondarily as replacements for carrier-based aircraft.

Having attack aviation as an integral part of the plan, reporting to the same commander, turned out to be a terrific way to conduct business, particularly when the proverbial poop hit that fabled propeller. Guadalcanal proved it; Henderson Field was so close to the fighting that Marine pilots were releasing ordnance in what amounted to the landing pattern. Once the field was secured, the planes provided an on-call close air support that could be brought to bear on any attack that the Japanese might make—and they made a *lot* of them. The F4F Wildcats and, later, F4U Corsairs could—as

"Fast-roping" is a technique used to rapidly insert Marines onto an objective. It is a favored technique for the hostage rescue teams that have become an integral part of the "special-operations-capable" Marine task forces because it can put a fire team on a rooftop in just a few seconds, much faster than rappelling.

An AV-8B Harrier waits for the signal to launch.

they say—put a world of hurt on the enemy, faster, more reliably than naval gunfire or Army aviation or even Marine artillery. The idea that aviation could make a Marine infantry unit much more effective was a theory in the very early sixties, a proven fact by the late sixties, and a fundamental part of doctrine ever since. As a result, the ACE usually has two types of jet fighters, four models of helicopters, and a mixed bag of fixed-wing aircraft dedicated to the mission. These aircraft provide air superiority and combat air patrol, close air support, air assault troop lifts, logistics support, and add mobility to artillery and other combat assets.

One of the things that made it work so well then—and so well now, too—is that there is a bond between the guy in the plane and the guy on the ground. Part of that bond is formal, structural, an extenuation of the chain of command. But part of it is that business of heritage and tradition, the Marine mystique that keeps coming up in discussions. A Marine company commander on the ground knows that he can count on the Harrier driver overhead when things turn ugly. The Marine in the Harrier knows the company commander on the ground, as an individual quite often, as a member of a community always. The same kind of relationship simply doesn't exist with the other services' pilots; they may be friends

Capt "Tinker" Bell and Maj "Mace" Macak pause before launching their F/A-18D Hornet from Marine Corps Air Station (MCAS) El Toro, California.

Lt Alfred Cunningham, the first Marine aviator, in 1912.

A DH-4 attacks a rebel position in Nicaragua, 1927. Marines are credited with the invention of dive-bombing during this campaign at the battle with bandits in the town of Ocotal in July of 1927. The mission today uses faster aircraft and heavier weapons but the idea hasn't changed a bit. USMC

As the infantry moves up, Marine air provides close air support with some well-placed napalm on enemy positions in the distance.

and colleagues, but they aren't members of the family.

Part of being a member of the same family means that limitations and capabilities are better understood. The landing-force commander is a senior Marine officer who knows both Marine air and Marine ground communities from long association. As commander of both elements in the operation, he is in a much better position to use both efficiently and effectively than might be the case with, for example, Air Force or Army assets.

ACE Mission

The primary mission of Marine air today, as for the last fifty-plus years, is to support

Marine ground operations. The secondary mission is to support the fleet as part of the Naval force. This is a complicated business with many kinds of aircraft, missions, and functions. The ACE commander is subordinate to the CLF. Here's what the ACE has to provide:

Offensive air support. Offensive air support goes after enemy air and ground targets that immediately threaten the landing force. This is the work of fighter aircraft, the "fast-movers" like the F/A-18 Hornet and AV-8 Harrier. Marine doctrine splits the offensive air doctrine into two quite different responsibilities: close air support and deep air support.

Close air support. The close-air-support mission is the big-payoff one for Marine air. It is an air-to-ground attack mission that is usually executed close to Marine (or allied)

ground forces in contact with an enemy. Close air support is the "glory" mission for Marine aviators because it requires an extremely high degree of skill to put bombs and bullets effectively on an enemy who may only be a hundred meters from Marines. It demands close coordination with the Marine ground units, normally through a forward air controller (FAC), a Marine pilot who accompanies ground combat units. Close air support is currently the primary job for the AV-8 Harrier and the AH-1 Cobra.

When Desert Storm kicked off, the AV-8 Harrier IIs from Cherry Point, North Carolina, and Yuma, Arizona, were along to provide close air support. Operating from ships and forward, austere bases, the AV-8B turned out to be another of the many systems that had been ripped apart by the popular news media only to perform just as advertised when push came to shove. Primary missions were against enemy artillery, armor, troop concentrations, convoys, and supply dumps. About 3,400 combat sorties were flown during the six weeks of operations against the Iraqis, delivering almost six million pounds of bombs, rockets, missiles, and bullets.

The first mission was flown as the curtain came up on Act One, 17 January 1991. An OV-10 Bronco patrolling near the border town of

Bringing out the wounded, Korea. The Corps pioneered (but didn't invent) helicopter support for military operations. The helicopter is an HRS-1 Sikorsky, equally effective at bringing up ammunition and hot food as well as evacuating wounded to hospitals in the rear. USMC by S/Sgt M. McMahon

Harriers aboard Belleau Wood, *ready to taxi.*

Capt. Dave Bonner, VMA-231, MCAS Cherry Point, North Carolina.

Ras al Khafji reported artillery rounds impacting on the abandoned town and the refinery nearby. Harriers from Marine Attack Squadron 311 (VMA-311, the "Tomcats") from MCAS Yuma were set up nearby and were called in by the FAC, The AV-8s provided the combat trial for the B-model by delivering 1,000-pound iron bombs on the artillery batteries that were doing the shooting from just across the border. All the guns were knocked out.

Harriers were airborne for the rest of the war, around the clock. Since they were based close to the fight there was no need for the long sorties, the in-flight refueling, or the external fuel tanks that were needed by conventional fighter-bomber aircraft. The Harrier proved to be reliable, with a mission-capable rate of about 90 percent, and efficient, with "combat turns" of about thirty minutes for refuel and rearm. Most of the aircraft operated from a base inside a soccer stadium but one squadron flew from an amphibious assault ship in the Persian Gulf.

"We accelerate faster to a slow air speed than any other airplane in the inventory," says one Harrier pilot, with a smirk. Slow in this case is about 400 knots, and is fast enough. The Harrier does a lot of things better than other airplanes—another example of the past driving the present. The AV-8B is a goofy design from a traditional perspective, all funny angles and shapes. Part of that comes from its English heritage—they seem to have a different solution to the problems of aerodynamics over there—but part comes from its mission. The Harrier is a drop-dead-gorgeous close-air-support airplane, dedicated to putting some serious hurt on the loyal opposition.

To do that mission the Marine Corps has applied the lessons of World War II, Korea, and Vietnam (those ghosts again). One of those lessons was that it is important to have your close air support assets—the airplanes and pilots that will arrive overhead when things get ugly on the ground—completely dedicated, part of the same team. Now, it used to be that the Air Force and Navy were supposed to fulfill this mission, and they did, too—when it was convenient. But they had other missions, other priorities, and other loyalties. The close-air-support mission is dangerous. There is no easy way to put bombs, rockets, or bullets accurately on the bad guys without getting down there and mixing with them. Even then it can be difficult to see the target. And anytime you get below about 10,000 feet you become vulnerable to anti-aircraft guns and heat-seeking missiles.

There are several ways to deal with enemy air defenses. One is to stay away; that's what happened a lot in World War II and Vietnam. Another is to dedicate part of the force to close air support and make them accountable for it; that's what the Marine Corps did with the Harrier and with the Cobra.

The AV-8B is being upgraded with a FLIR (forward looking infra-red) sensor suite that permits night attack missions to be flown with improved accuracy. The new aircraft have improved cockpit displays and ergonomics. A digital, moving-map display is one of the things that will help with the close-air-support mission. The APG-65 radar is also being fitted to the Harrier for better air-to-air, all-weather mission performance. This new, radar-equipped Harrier will be called the Harrier II Plus.

Harrier Mission

Although the cockpit may appear intimidating, the aircraft is extremely easy to start and to operate in combat—compared to earlier systems. Here's how it works:

First, you need to dress for the occasion. That means Nomex underwear, standard Nomex flight suit, anti-g suit ("speed jeans"), survival equipment vest, parachute harness, boots, and flight helmet. Properly fitted the harness makes it difficult to walk, so leave the leg straps unfastened until you're ready to climb the ladder.

Although the crew chief will have checked everything carefully, you're responsible for the airplane once you sign the book, so a preflight inspection is not only required, its a good idea. Start at the boarding ladder and work your

The AV-8 Harrier II is a British-designed fighter built by McDonnell Douglas. Although quite complex, it is a marvelously agile and adept aircraft, perfectly suited to the Marine close-air-support mission. The Harrier lacks radar and it is not designed for the counter-air mission, although it can defend itself well if necessary. Its angle-rate bombing system and excellent fire-control computer make it an extremely accurate platform for delivery of bombs, rockets, and cannon fire. And its ability to take off and land from any weed patch, dirt road, or tennis court means the Harrier can be based near the Marine infantry units that it supports.

way around, looking for anything loose, broken, bent, leaking, damaged, or missing. Then sign the book to accept the aircraft, climb aboard, and settle in.

The crew chief will have configured all the cockpit switches for a quick getaway, but you should check them against the checklist anyway. Start at the back of the left panel, sweep around to the right, and verify the position of every control. There is a "built-in test" panel; run the BITs and one of the aircraft computers will investigate the health of every major system aboard and give you a report on the multi-function display.

The crew chief will help you buckle the harness connectors to the ejection seat; it is difficult to reach the two lower ones, so the assist is welcome. You have to attach the lanyards for the leg restraints yourself; in an ejection your feet will be pulled back against the seat to help prevent "flail" injuries.

You start the engine by simply switching on battery power. The panel is over by your right knee; move the BAT switch to ON. About three inches to the left is the START switch; move it to the ON position and you'll hear the engine start to spin. The engine RPM is displayed on a little screen at the lower center of the front panel; when the indicator starts to

The Harrier cockpit. The AV-8 currently lacks radar although it will be included in the II Plus when it enters service.

A pod of 5-inch Zuni rockets are loaded aboard an AV-8B Harrier at MCAS Yuma, Arizona. These big, accurate, extremely powerful rockets have been a part of the warload of Marine close-air-support aircraft since World War II. These particular rockets have been around nearly that long; they've been waiting for this moment since the early 1970s. Outboard of the rocket pod, and not shown in the photograph, is a Sidewinder missile with a yellow rubber cover protecting its delicate seeker head.

94

show rotation (3 percent is a safe speed), advance the throttle from STOP to IDLE. The rest is completely automatic—at 11 percent RPM the fuel begins to flow, the flame is lit, and the engine will spin up to idle RPM. "In a combat situation," one pilot says, " with a good ground crew and an experienced pilot you can be airborne in five minutes. And that's the way the Harrier was designed, to be a quick-reaction platform to support the Marines on the ground."

Once the engine starts you are essentially in business. There is a post-start checklist to run through, and then you can taxi. A normal combat mission will require you to have entered mission data into the mission system computer and have the inertial navigation system "initialized," a process that takes several minutes but that can be done well in advance of engine start, while the aircraft is sitting on the ramp in "alert" status on battery power.

With taxi clearance, it's now a good time to complete the pre-combat checklist. This could be done in the air, but there never seems to be enough time once you're airborne, so most pilots do them on the ground, if time per-

Under the control of the yellow-shirted deck handlers, a Harrier glides across the flight deck to a holding position. It will be inspected by a horde of *Navy flight-deck specialists before being directed to the centerline and launched into space.*

mits. Then comes the pre-takeoff checks: arm the ejection seat, set the flaps to STOL (short take off/landing), nozzle stop set—fifty-five degrees is typical. Once you're cleared for takeoff, position the nozzles full aft and monitor the engine on the multi-function display while you advance the power from 27 to 55 percent. Bring the nozzles back to the stops and check for flap extension—it happens automatically, most of the time. The water switch is armed; water will be injected as soon as you exceed 95 percent. Duct pressure should indicate about fifty PSI, and you're set to go. The HUD (head-up display) will indicate nozzle angle and

power settings. Advance the throttle to MIL power, up to the throttle stop and you'll start your takeoff roll. The HUD will cue you to rotate the nozzle based on data you've preprogrammed, a critical air speed: slam the nozzle control back to the stop, in this case fifty-five degrees, and you will promptly become unstuck. Pull the nose up; fourteen degrees will give you a max rate short takeoff climb-out. Once you establish a positive rate of climb, start rotating the nozzles aft (twenty degrees is about right for the moment) and bring up the gear, switch the flaps from STOL to AUTO, turn off the water injection and dese-

That keypad allows you to enter all kinds of flight and weapons data into the Harrier's computers be-

fore and during flight. Much of the cockpit management routine is improved tremendously as a result.

lect the COMBAT switch that provides a little extra heat for the engine.

In a real-world combat situation, you don't just go off and do battle. There are probably dozens or maybe hundreds of other aircraft zipping to and fro, so you will be under departure control. In fact, you probably get to talk to several controllers on the way to the target area before you can call up the FAC, who will assign you your target. He can be in an F/A-18, an OV-1, or on the ground; regardless, he's a Marine aviator who knows both your aircraft's capabilities and the needs of the guys on the ground. Wherever he is, he is close to the action and has eyes on the target. You've got his frequency plugged into the computer; push a button and report in: tell him your mission number, call sign, aircraft type, how many in your flight, what's on the bomb racks, and how long you plan to stick around. You

say, "Kilo One Two, this is Hammer One One: Now at CP [Control Point], over."

The reply will be: "This is Kilo One Two: Request line-up, over."

"This is Hammer One One, mission number 1210027: I have two AV-8s, six Mavericks, and twenty mike-mike on each. On station for two zero minutes, over."

He'll say, "Roger." Then, when he's ready for you, he'll call, "Hammer One One, this is Kilo One Two: Ready to copy mission brief?"

If you are, key the mike and say, "Roger, Hammer One One is ready to copy."

The FAC reads the brief one line at a time; you punch it into the computer as you get it.

"Golf," he says (that's the initial point, the IP, a point on your map and his, a terrain-reference feature that you just can't miss; things start getting serious from the IP). "Three zero five right" (that's your heading from the IP

Vertical landings make a lot more sense than vertical take-offs. The latter consume a lot of fuel that is better used in extending the range of the mission,

carrying heavier bomb loads or adding to the already short loiter time.

97

and direction to the target). You will make a right turn to 305 degrees true at the IP. Key it in.

"One six," he says, telling you how far to the target—sixteen miles from the IP. Press 1 and 6 and ENT on the keypad.

"Three five zero," giving you the elevation of the target, important information if you expect the weapons computer to do its stuff with precision.

"Five tanks," giving you the target.

"Whisky Papa," specifying the type of ordnance you should use. (That's how you say "WP" in International Phonetic Alphabet, and "WP" is white phosphorus, an extremely nasty kind of ordnance that badly burns anything its little fragments touch. White phosphorus makes lots of pretty white smoke, though, and is very easy to see.)

"One thousand," giving you the distance in meters to the closest friendlies. If they were much closer he'd add, "Danger close."

The F/A-18D Hornet is a two-seat, dual-purpose fighter that is an essential part of the Marine arsenal. The Hornet isn't the fastest kid in town, but it has been called the finest fighter in the skies today. That's because it is extremely agile, is a true all-weather fighter and bomber, and has an integrated fire-control system that is extraordinarily accurate. It carries a tremendous load, operates from the Navy's carriers or austere expeditionary airfields across the beach, and is comparatively simple and straightforward to maintain. This one is owned and operated by VMFA (AW)-225, the "Vikings," who call MCAS El Toro home, and is flown by the unit's genial commander, Lt Col Jon Gallinetti. His friends call him "Goose," but you can call him "sir."

"Z-S-U twenty-three four, two kilometers northeast," telling you that a four-barrel, 23mm ZSU-23-4 antiaircraft battery is the closest threat the FAC knows about, but there may be others.

"Time to target, three plus zero zero. . . MARK!"

Get it all? Acknowledge by pressing the button and transmitting, "Roger."

The HUD starts counting down the seconds. At the appointed instant your airplane needs to be precisely over the IP to begin the run in to the target. The IP will be a crossroads or some other feature on the ground you can clearly identify. The mission computer provides navigation data that make this kind of precision practical.

A command-speed/time function of the computer will help put you over the target on time. Tell it where you are going and when you want to get there—it will tell you when to leave or it will tell you what airspeed to fly.

There is the IP ahead; time to call the FAC and tell him how its going: "Kilo One Two, this is Hammer One One: Approaching IP, over."

"Hammer One One, Kilo One Two: Roger," he replies. "You are cleared to depart IP. Report departing IP, over."

Once you push on out of the IP, you and your wingman will split, separating so that you don't get caught in his bomb pattern. You're making a low-angle attack in a sophisticated threat environment—watch your flight leader while he goes in, to see whether a hand-held surface-to-air missile comes up at him or whether a gun opens up on him. If your wingman is engaged by enemy fire, you'll be his only clue until he's inside a fireball because his attention is directed to the target and his mission. Your mission, for the moment, is to cover his ass.

"This is Hammer One One: Departing IP, over."

"Hammer One One, this is Kilo One Two: I have you in sight. Target is at your two o'clock, over."

You roll in, get cleared "hot" from the FAC

and switch the armament panel control from SAFE to ARM. The HUD will display the constantly computed aim point and release cues; in AUTO mode, the computer does everything except fly the airplane. You don't actually pickle the bombs off yourself, but by depressing the small red button on the top of the stick you "consent" to let the mission computer pop off the Mavericks at the appropriate instant.

"This is Hammer One One: Roger, over."

"This is Hammer One One: Laser on, over.

"This is Kilo One Two: Laser on, over."

A pair of "Deltas" cruise above the ragged Sierra Nevada—a notorious place to practice your survival skills.

"This is Hammer One One: I have the spot, over."

"This is Kilo One Two: You are cleared hot, over."

"Hammer One One, this is Kilo One Two: End of mission. T-62 tanks destroyed. You are released from control, over."

The previous mission employed high-tech Maverick laser-guided bombs, but a lot of bombing involves plain old Mk 82 iron bombs that just free-fall to the target. Although the

The D-models' cockpit is clean, uncluttered, and extremely functional. The "glass cockpit" uses a minimum of instruments to present a maximum of information by allowing a crew member to display only the information needed at the moment, on command.

computer can pop them off when it thinks they should leave, most Marine Harrier drivers prefer to do their own releasing; so the most popular method of bombing uses the constantly computed impact point. That mode provides a "velocity vector" bomb fall line with a little cross at the bottom displayed in the HUD. All you have to do is fly the cross over the target and push the button. "Although there are other ways to deliver bombs," says one pilot, "we definitely prefer computed bombing. Even an inexperienced pilot can consistently deliver bombs to within thirty feet from any kind of delivery. We had a guy make three deliveries here recently, all hit inside ten feet! The system is real good."

Flight lead will keep an eye on you, and if anything ugly comes up in your direction he'll probably let you know. With the bombs off, bring the stick back in your lap and jink away, making it hard for the enemy to puncture you or the crew chief's airplane. The pull-out will probably be a six or seven G-load, squishing you down in the seat and making the speed jeans inflate for a moment.

Okay, time to go home. There are five ways to take off and five ways to land. It's possible to land conventionally, but since the plane wants to keep flying all the way down to an airspeed of about forty knots, it isn't a lot of fun. Another alternative is to rotate the nozzle to a set position and fly it in that way; or, when you are bringing back a lot of bombs and it's hot or high, you can use a variable nozzle position approach. As one pilot explains, "The vertical landing is something unique—in the fixed-wing community—to the Harrier. We come into the overhead as a flight-of-two, 350 knots' airspeed, do a four- or five-G 'break' maneuver like any other fighter to bleed off the airspeed quickly. As soon as we see 350 knots, flaps go to STOL and that drives the flaps down to twenty-five degrees. That slows the airplane down in a hurry and it starts getting noisy and squirrelly. At 250 knots the gear lever goes down; when the indicators all go green the nozzle goes back to fifty degrees, water switch to TAKEOFF, slam the power up and monitor for clean acceleration, then switch to LAND mode. As you slow through 150 knots, bam, the flaps come down to sixty-two degrees—big barn doors sticking out there."

At about 2,500 feet you hit a point in the approach called the "key" and the nozzle comes back to the "hover stop"—about 82 degrees; there's no forward thrust now, you are floating like a big, expensive hockey puck. Now you use the thrusters to provide directional control—it's automatic; the throttle controls rate of descent. You fly yourself down to about 150 feet, stabilize for a moment, then continue to fifty feet and set up your visual cues for alignment with the pad, reduce the power a little and make little check turns to control any drift. One thing that takes a long time to learn about the Harrier is that there is a little delay in the hover between control input and reaction that isn't present in conventional aircraft. Using very slight throttle modulation, you continue the descent. Once the main gear touch the deck, bring the power all the way back to IDLE. You have, as they say, cheated death again!

Missions

Marine air flies a wide variety of missions besides close air support. The big one in the

The cathode-ray-tube screens are called multi-function displays. You can choose engine data, a moving map, weapons information, a mission checklist, *navigation data, the HUD display and the radar, as appropriate.*

Gulf was deep air support. The deep-air-support mission attacks enemy targets that are not immediately engaged with friendly forces: tanks moving toward the battlefield, troop concentrations, communications facilities, and rail yards or bridges in the rear. Deep air support is done safely away from friendly ground forces, beyond what is called the "fire support coordination line." Harriers and Hornets fly these missions.

Another mission is called assault support and consists of trucking things and people around the battlefield. This mission is typical-ly executed by the cargo helicopters and C-130 transport airplanes. Assault support assists the commander and the ground-maneuver elements by making things move faster and easier. Helicopters are used to deliver assault forces over the beach, airlifting Marines directly into combat. The mission also includes delivering cargo, with both fixed- and rotary-wing aircraft, to the combat elements. It provides air evacuation of the combat units in an emergency, and it includes air refueling from Marine C-130 tankers. But most of the assault-support mission is done with helicopters.

The helicopter was of little interest to the Air Force after World War II, but the Army and Marines both saw some potential in the early machines. The Marine Corps started using them in Korea, with great success. Even the little H-13 could quickly deliver a few hundred pounds of critical supplies and ammunition to a forward-deployed infantry unit in combat in locations where mules would fear to tread. And the little helicopter could take the wounded out, too, and have them at an aid station or hospital in time to save a life that would have previously been lost.

By the time Marines started fighting in Vietnam, the Corps was the proud owner of quite a few H-34 helicopters, each powerful enough to carry a squad of infantry (on a good day). In fact, Marines were fighting in Vietnam in 1963—and dying, too—even though many chronologies say that the American part of that war didn't begin until two years later.

Antiair Warfare

The second major mission for the ACE is a defensive one, protecting the landing force from enemy air threats. The ACE defends against enemy fighters, ground attack aircraft, bombers, and missiles with its own interceptors, bombers, anti-aircraft guns, and SAMs—plus electronic warfare systems—all in an effort to gain and maintain air superiority. The counter-air mission is active and passive. The ACE can launch missions against enemy aircraft, airfields, missile sites, radars, and air defense systems.

A "Whiskey" and water. The Cobra has been through a lot of changes since it came into service almost thirty years ago. The current AH-1W version has twin engines for survivability, speed, and power, and can fire the excellent Hellfire missile. It is an economical, efficient alternative to the Army's very expensive Apache; some Army aviators think the Marines made the right choice.

Combat Air Patrol and the Hornet

The F/A-18 Hornet doesn't look like a loser, but it sort of is. The design was originally the YF-17, a competitor for an air-superiority fighter for the Air Force; the F-16 Falcon—the Electric Jet—won that one, but the Hornet did so well in the evaluations that it survived. Lucky thing, too, because it has turned into a star performer for both the Navy and Marines, for Canada, and for other nations.

There are two versions: single seat and dual seat. The latter is the much more capable night-attack Delta model. It's small, by fighter standards: about thirty-eight feet from one wing tip to the other, but with two engines pumping out 8,000 pounds of thrust each it will move along pretty smartly. The D-model uses the latest "glass cockpit" and HOTAS (hands on throttle and stick) approach to cockpit ergonomics and that means that important chores, like navigation and weapons delivery, are a bit easier than with older "steam gauge" technologies of the past. That doesn't mean the pilot's life is any easier but that they now ask him to do more.

It's not the fastest plane on the block, but with a top speed of Mach 1.8, it can move right along. Actually, the top speeds published for

If the CH-46 is the Marines' pickup truck, the CH-53 is the White Freightliner of helicopters. This huge beast will haul 32,000 pounds, has a combat radius of fifty miles with that payload, and can operate from ships over the horizon. It will lift the big 155mm howitzer, trucks, vehicles, and can recover downed aircraft. The blades fold—but only when they aren't turning; that makes it much more compact, allowing several to be stowed aboard ships of the Tarawa class.

fighter aircraft are quite misleading. They are true enough—for an aircraft without any bombs or missiles aboard, and with a minimum of fuel, too. The important factors don't fit neatly into the data sheets: How easy is it to get where you're supposed to be, when you're supposed to be there; how long can you loiter in the target area; how well can you see the other guy? Air combat starts at high speeds but dogfights use it up in a hurry. Long-range engagements may be desirable, but they are easy to defeat. Acceleration is probably more important than top speed—a pilot wants to add all the energy possible to a Sidewinder before firing it, so he'll go into "burner" just before launch.

As wonderful an aircraft as the Hornet is, in many ways the MiGs and Sukhois that op-

Need a lift?

posed them over Iraq and Kuwait are superior airplanes and (in the hands of a competent combat pilot) extremely dangerous adversaries. Now that the Russians are allowing Western observers to study and fly their best combat aircraft we've made a startling discovery—they are more agile, faster accelerating, and have detection systems that have real advantages over American ones, and missiles that are at least as capable as the ones on Western aircraft. The difference, of course, can't be included on any list of specifications because it is the quality of the flight crew that is the most important part of any weapon system. Marine pilots are trained to an extremely high standard in very realistic combat exercises; their adversaries in the Gulf were grossly incompetent pilots flying excellent and dangerous fighters.

Flying in the Hornet is, like flying in the Harrier, a treat. The cockpit is tight; you don't really get into it, you put it on. The clean multi-function displays put information in front of you in an efficient, uncluttered way. Engine start is automatic and a pretty much brainless routine. Even taxing out to the blocks the airplane feels tight, strong, and agile, and it motors along at a good clip; the feel is Ferrari-like, expensive, delicious, state-of-the-art. Out at the departure end of the runway, with takeoff clearance, you and your wingman make a section takeoff. Flight lead nods his head—the cue to release breaks and advance the throttle all the way forward into afterburner. The roar of the engine rises to vibrate you. Acceleration at first is smooth and deliberate but hardly stunning. Then the afterburner lights off and you receive a solid push from the ejection seat and the runway streams past, a blur. About ten seconds of burner will get you to 150 knots. A little back pressure on the stick will tilt the nose up, and there will suddenly be a lot of air between your gear and the ground. Come back out of burner and you'll sag forward against the harness as you decelerate. The gear comes up. Flight lead is about a quarter-mile ahead, climbing through the ragged clouds at about

3,000 feet per minute—a mild, economical departure.

On top of the weather you close up on your leader. A good combat formation will have you on line about a mile apart for mutual support—they learned that one fifty years ago, over the Pacific, against the Japanese, and it still works.

The Hornet gets an F/A designation because it gets used for fighter missions and attack missions. The FLIR sensor provides a thermal picture of the ground below, even at night and in bad weather, that makes the D-model Hornet a great close-air-support plane and a deep-interdiction platform as well. The FLIR is mostly the wizzo's (slang for the Weapons System Officer, or WSO, the backseater who operates the radar and other equipment while the pilot flies the airplane) toy, but he can put the display up on the HUD for the pilot's amusement, when appropriate. And that's when it's time to drop iron on something late at night or in the clouds.

Although the "battlefield preparation" mission doesn't have the same glory as air-to-air combat, the effect on the ground war can be just as great. The only Marine who scored an air-to-air kill in the Gulf war did it in an Air Force F-15. But the effect of all the bombs dropped on artillery positions, on ammo dumps, and on supply columns had a lot to do with the rapid victory during the ground phase of the campaign. In fact, Desert Storm's air campaign was the first time combat aviation has fully delivered on its old promise, going back to Billy Mitchell and other prophets from the 1920s, that airplanes could be decisive in war. It wasn't true in World War II, Korea, or Vietnam, but it was finally true in the Gulf.

The CH-46 Sea Knight is the faithful pickup truck for the Corps, delivering people, weapons, food, ammunition, and all the other supplies required by a task force far from home. They are old, loud, high-mileage aircraft that entered service about thirty years ago and may be around for another decade or two.

Cobra

The AH-1W Cobra helicopter, believe it or not, is actually a bastard child of the tubby old UH-1 Huey. Back in the military dark ages, during the war in Vietnam, the close-air-support mission was one of the weakest links in anybody's bag of tricks. The Navy and Air Force jets (designed strictly for dogfights) were too fast to really see the targets—on those rare occasions when they could find a hole in the clouds and came down to support the troops. And the Huey gunships, an improvised solution, turned out to be an antiaircraft gunner's dream come true: a fat, slow, vulnerable single-engine target that was easy to bag. For a while, World War II-surplus propeller air-

planes performed the mission, but they got used up. Helicopters had many virtues in that war, and so a requirement for an attack version was written. After many months and a very expensive failure, a design based on the Huey was flown. The Cobra is essentially a Huey with tandem seating for two, some armor, a gun, and pods for rockets. The gunner sits up front where he can see better. The skinny little airframe, the armor, and all those rockets and bullets made for a potent little package. The early ones, fully loaded, could hardly get out of their own way and had a range of about five miles. But those little deficiencies were quickly fixed, and the Cobra started arriving overhead when Marine in-

A CH-53 on the road again with another load of groceries and ammunition for the happy campers ashore.

fantry companies bumped into trouble and began biting the Viet Cong with 20mm fangs.

The exterior of today's AH-1W Cobra is nearly identical to that of the old model, but most of the interior details have been improved. The Whiskey version is the most recent in a long line of enhancements, complete with two engines, a stabilized sight for the gun and racks for the superb Hellfire anti-armor missiles. The two engines allow it to hover out of ground effect at 3,500 feet with a full load of missiles and fuel aboard, something the first Cobra couldn't do at sea level, in ground effect.

Of all the lessons learned from the Gulf war, one certainly must be the value of stand-off weapons like the Hellfire when used on an agile platform like the Cobra. The Whisky's mobility, night vision sights and sensors, and the long range of the missile meant that tanks and artillery could be engaged at ranges much farther than the enemy's weapons could return fire. Even if the Iraqi tankers could have seen the Cobras (which they usually couldn't) their tank main guns were out-ranged by the Hellfires. And the Hellfire is a spectacularly accurate weapon that relies on a laser designator for targeting at ranges of up to about three and a half miles; a tank's main gun is good out to about half that.

The battle around Khafji on the night of 29–30 January was the first clue that American military planners had that maybe everything was going to work out as planned. When the Iraqis came blasting down the coast road, the Whiskeys were in the air in less than an hour. Despite the darkness, they identified friendly forces in the town, even though they'd been told there were none. The Iraqi armor was sorted out and destroyed with Hellfire and TOW missiles, guns, and rockets. This was first blood for the Whiskey model, and it was the first success against armor and artillery targets for the coalition, too.

The Cobras continued to perform superbly throughout the preliminaries and the big event as well. Just before the big show, the Marines got into a substantial fight along the Kuwait border. Recon elements from 2nd Light Armored Infantry Battalion, poking deep into the enemy side of the frontier, were engaged by artillery, armor, and small arms. On the third day of the recon a force of over twenty Iraqi tanks appeared. The LAVs engaged with everything they had—which wasn't too much. The 25mm rounds from the chain gun pecked ineffectually at the hide of the enemy armor. Then, the Cobras waded in with Hellfires and the tanks were rapidly engaged and destroyed.

Air Assault

One of the enduring lessons of many wars is the value of mobility. In fact, mobility is built right into the Marine's basic mission as a component of the fleet. Marines have traditionally gotten into trouble when immobilized one way or another. In World War I, World War II, Korea, and Vietnam that has happened when Marines units have been used in static ways, or in ways that violated the basic charter of the Corps. That charter involves movement and a kind of agility that strikes and withdraws, hits and moves away. Whenever Marines have had to hit somebody and then stay put (Belleau Wood, Iwo Jima, Chosin Reservoir, Khe Sahn), the mission gets accomplished but at a tremendous cost in Marine lives.

Around 1963, Marines operating out of Da Nang, up in the I Corps area of South Vietnam, were giving rides out to the country for selected members of the Vietnamese military. The rides were in CH-34 helicopters, big enough for a whole squad of the smaller South Vietnamese troops and an American advisor or two. The helicopters could take a company of these troops out and drop them off in a rice paddy, far from any road, and right out of the blue. If you happened to be a member of the Viet Cong guerrillas this could be quite bothersome. It was even more bothersome when the helicopters brought T-28 fighter escorts because then you could hardly put your head up to take a shot at the visitors without inviting a couple of 2.75-inch rockets or .50-caliber machine-gun fire on your position. When the South Vietnamese soldiers actually felt like fighting (which was sometimes, but not always) such air assaults could be extremely effective.

In 1965, the Marines (at the suggestion of President Lyndon Johnson) decided they could do the job better themselves and started flying a lot of air-assault missions. The helicopter turned out to be a terrific addition to the Marine bag of tricks. It could drop a company of Marines into some of the darndest spots, let them roam around for a while, annoying the natives, then come and get them later. As new turbine-powered designs, with tremendous power, light weight, and vastly improved reliability, came into service, the possibilities seemed endless.

CH-46

The CH-46 Sea Knight helicopter arrived for duty in 1965, powerful enough to carry a couple of squads or a M101 105mm howitzer and some ammunition. One of the things it could do was to put the infantry in the paddies and put a few artillery tubes on some convenient hilltop nearby; then when the poop hit the propeller (which, of course, was the basic idea), the artillery was just a phone call away. The poor VC were receiving one unpleasant

The gold wings of a naval aviator. Marine and Navy pilots attend the same schools and wear the same insignia. Marine aviation is essentially a small, full-service air force dedicated to supporting *amphibious operations ashore—particularly the young riflemen out in the weeds who are the pointy end of the spear.*

surprise after another: Marines appearing in their previously safe backyard, and instead of a nice, fair, infantry-to-infantry fight, the American team arrives with the heavy fire support. It probably seemed very unfair—and that was perfectly okay with the Marines.

The air assault was developed into a military version of an art form in the middle sixties by the Army and the Marines—along with the Soviets, the Brits, and others too. For Marines it was (and still is) based on the lift capability of the CH-46 to carry people, ammunition, food, casualties, and just about anything else that will fit from ship to shore and beyond.

The CH-46 Sea Knight has been improved over the years. It is rated at a top speed of 166 miles per hour and a range of 190 nautical miles. It has two gun stations, each mounting .50-caliber heavy machine guns. There is room for seventeen Marines or 4,200 pounds of cargo inside or out. The back ramp will drop, allowing Marines to jump, "fast-rope," or rappel out; they can also come back aboard by climbing an air-assault ladder that can be lowered to the ground, or Special Purpose Insertion and Extraction System (SPIES) rigged on the end of a long, strong rope.

CH-53

The Sea Knight was great, but Marines wanted something even bigger. It arrived in the form of the huge CH-53 Sea Stallion heli-copter, the biggest rotary-wing aircraft outside Russia. It will haul 32,000 pounds of anything either inside or on its two external cargo hooks. It has seating for fifty-five guests, whose needs are attended to by a friendly, attentive staff of three, two pilots and an air crewman. It will cruise along at about 170 knots and will go about 500 nautical miles on a tank of gas. And, since it is a Marine helicopter, it is designed to go to sea and can land on the flight decks of many of the Navy's ships, although it looks out of place on many of them. The Sea Stallion's bulk is reduced considerably by some special features of its design: the blades fold back, and the tail rotor pylon folds up in a way that converts the helicopter from something immense to something of manageable size.

It, too, goes back to about 1965, when it entered service. Its primary mission was to provide heavy lift to support amphibious assaults by carrying heavy artillery and priority vehicles from ship to shore. The troop-lift capability was a bonus, not an essential.

They don't do it often, and never with troops aboard, but pilots actually have looped and rolled the huge helicopter—a maneuver that would rip the blades right off a lesser design.

During the years it was deployed to Southeast Asia, Marine Heavy Helicopter Squadron 463 used the CH-53 to recover almost 1,100 downed airplanes. Nine were lost in combat and another ten in accidents.

Chapter 6

A Short History of the Corps

The history of the Corps is far too rich and detailed to be given justice in a book of this size. There are many books dedicated to the subject, some of which are included in the appendix. But this history is also too important to ignore here, because there are so many lessons for contemporary Marines in the successes and disasters of the past. Marines, unlike members of other services, are expected to study history and apply it. In fact, the Commandant publishes a reading list every year with a list of titles for all Marines to study and discuss.

When the United States was founded it was—and still largely is—with a pacifist, isolationist point of view. The Army and Navy were temporary institutions, invented for the Revolutionary War, disbanded after. For a time, the only real combat force defending the new nation was the Coast Guard's tiny sloops and miniature guns.

But events have a nasty way of imposing decisions on people and institutions, and that's what happened almost immediately after Independence. Although France had been an ally against the English, tensions developed and a kind of war with French pirates soon began. In 1794 the Congress had authorized the construction of six new warships, including *Constitution, Constellation,* and *United States*. In 1795 the United States was forced to sign a humiliating treaty with Algiers and to pay a million dollar tribute; there was, at the time, no alternative. In 1796 and 1797 American merchant captains were forced to ransom themselves and their vessels from various predators at sea. In 1798 came an authorization for Marines to serve aboard the new vessels:

"Resolved, That, in addition to the present Military Establishment, there shall be raised a battalion, to be called the Marine Corps, to consist of a Major, and suitable commissioned and non-commissioned officers, five hundred privates, and the necessary musicians, including the Marines now in service; and the Marines which shall be employed in the armed vessels and galleys of the United States shall be detachments from this corps."

The result, at first, was not very impressive. Recruiting standards were just a bit lower than at present. Uniforms, weapons, training, logistic support, and leadership standards were, by today's standards, often very bad, usually the result of an officer corps that could be quite casual about its responsibilities.

There's always one in every squad, but since he's been wounded we'll assume a brief rest was probably authorized by his "Gunny," as gunnery sergeants are called. These Marines are practicing their marksmanship skills against targets that shoot back. The range is in the Philippines, the occasion is just another little insurgency, this one in 1900. USMC

Some units were in disastrous shape, as one observer noted in 1799 after inspecting the Marine contingent aboard the USS *Philadelphia*: "I think it is not possible to produce such a shabby set of animals in this world."

The new American Navy went off to settle some scores and caught up with the French in the Caribbean. French ships were captured, and the guns of French fortresses ashore were spiked. It was the beginning of a trend. Marines helped the Navy fight a series of little wars during those early years, with pirates and diverse other scum, anywhere that American merchant shipping was threatened. The expression "sea lines of communication" didn't exist back then, but the idea was well understood.

The first expedition was against the Barbary pirates in the Mediterranean. O'Bannon's little force was fought in only one of many encounters between 1801 and 1815. Even so,

Raising the flag over Vera Cruz, Mexico, 1914. USMC

First Sergeant Dan Daly wears two Medals of Honor (and a Navy Cross), the only enlisted Marine so far to achieve the honor. The first came from the Boxer Rebellion when Daly held an exposed and vital position alone, under fire. The second was earned in Haiti when he retrieved his unit's only machine gun (again, under fire) from a river where it was lost during an engagement. USMC

there were only ten officers and about five hundred men in the force when war against England was declared in 1812. British naval ships had the bad manners to stop American vessels on the high seas and remove American sailors, forcing them to serve on English warships—and there wasn't a thing the young nation could do about it until the young American Navy was fit for sea.

The English had scorned the American Navy at the outset. But the British fleet quickly lost battles and ships to the upstarts from the former colonies. *Constitution*, *United States*, *Wasp*, and *Essex* pounded the stuffing out of a succession of English ships in the Atlantic; then *Essex* went off to the Pacific and did the same to British whalers. During these battles Marines used rifles and primitive hand grenades to keep the enemy ship's decks cleared during the close-range gun battles of the time, and went over the rail with sabers and pistols when the time came to board. It was a messy business, hand-to-hand combat with the sailors and Marines of the enemy.

The war lasted for three years, and the Marines distinguished themselves ashore and afloat, although their numbers were tiny and they were engaged not only with the British but against pirates in the Caribbean, too. They made up for their small numbers by being highly mobile, much more so than the larger Army, thanks to the transport of the Navy. Their work ashore and afloat marked them as an efficient, effective force worth preserving.

The Navy and Marine team proved useful for suppressing pirates and slave traders after the war, and later against the Seminole Indians in Florida. War with Mexico followed in 1846, and Marines once again proved themselves as infantry ashore, far from ships and the sea, leading the charge into Chapultepec castle and helping win California.

The nineteenth century was a busy one for the little Corps. There were frequent excursions to sunny, steamy ports of call around the world. Marines were showing up in some of the darnedest places—Panama, China, Nicaragua, Peru, Cuba, and Fiji—showing the flag and establishing order.

In 1859 John Brown staged an abortive slave uprising with the momentary capture of the US arsenal at Harpers Ferry, Virginia. An army officer named Robert E. Lee put down the rebellion and captured Brown—with a force of US Marines. During the assault on the building where the rebels were holding out, one of the Marine officers used his Mameluke

They called Smedley Butler "Old Gimlet Eye," but not to his face. He, like Dan Daly, won two Medals of Honor during a long career. He tried to turn one of them down as undeserved, but was out-ranked on the issue and had to wear it anyway. USMC

Projecting power ashore, Cape Gloucester. This is where amphibious assault theory was tried and tested—found wanting in places, successful in others. The United States was and still is the only nation able to execute large scale operations of this type.

sword (patterned after O'Bannon's) in an attempt to kill Brown; the sword broke, and Brown survived to be hung later.

During the Civil War, Marines played their traditional role of shipboard police, but didn't participate in the large land battles to the extent that they had before or would later. But as soon as the war was over, the Army was reduced to its usual small force and the Marine Corps served its traditional role of force projection abroad.

Between the Civil War and World War I the tiny Corps was kept busy around the globe, particularly in Central America and the Far East. The Marines brought civilization to a wide variety of heathen nations, whether they wanted it or not. Marines were handy, hardy, and businesslike. It didn't take much more than a grizzled old "gunny" and a platoon or so of Marines to suppress the kind of insurrections that were popular back then.

World War II

World War II started with the conclusion of World War I, but the bombs didn't start to fall until 0800, Sunday morning, 7 December 1941. Marine and Navy installations across the Pacific were attacked by carrier-based Japanese aircraft, with impressive results. American forces were hit hard, and not just at Pearl Harbor, but at Midway, Wake, Johnston, Palmyra, and Guam. It has been so long that the effect of these attacks has been almost forgotten. In fact, we nearly lost the war at the outset.

Surprise was virtually complete. Allied forces—British, Dutch, American—were devastated and in retreat or were dead. Marine Air Group 21 (MAG-21), at Ewa on Oahu lost every airplane in the initial attack, on the ground, without firing a shot. But Marines scrounged every weapon they could, including the guns in the destroyed aircraft, to return fire. Four Marines from the group died in the lopsided battle. One hundred twelve died at Pearl Harbor that morning. Six thousand Japanese soldiers landed on Guam and promptly defeated the 150 Marines opposing them.

But Wake Island, 1,000 miles to the west of Pearl Harbor, held out. Four hundred and fifty Marines arrived just before the shooting started, but they fought off an amphibious assault by a Japanese task force of about 1,000 men. Two enemy destroyer-transports, the *Hayate* and *Kisaragi*, were sent to the bottom by combined air and shore bombardment. It would be the sole victory for United States forces during 1941. The US Commander in Chief, Pacific asked by radio what the Marines needed, and a Marine radio operator replied, "Send us more Japs!" They came soon enough, on 23 December, this time overwhelming the defenders just as a relief force approached, too late.

It was a horrifying time for Americans, perhaps worst for all those who promoted appeasement and pacifism in the years preceding. Defeat and dishonor were everywhere: Hong Kong fell, then Singapore, the Philippines, and the "impregnable" fortress at Corregidor. In Europe as well as the Pacific the Axis powers appeared both tremendously evil and equally irresistible.

The tide began to turn in the Spring of 1942 at Midway Island. Through a combination of luck, good intelligence, and an excellent plan, a large Japanese task force was caught and beaten back by Navy and Marine aviators.

Guadalcanal

On 7 August 1942, 10,000 Marines executed America's first large amphibious operation by going ashore on Guadalcanal in the Solomon Islands. The landing was almost unopposed, and the first objective, a new air field, was captured the following day complete with large supplies of aviation fuel, rice, and engineering equipment. Although the landing was unopposed, the Japanese came back with a vengeance on the night of the eighth, sinking four American and Australian cruisers and chasing the invasion fleet away with much of the Marines' supplies and equipment still aboard. Then the Japanese counterattacked with forces landed on the north side of the island by regular arrivals of the "Tokyo Express," fast transports that efficiently delivered soldiers and supplies to the battle. There was a lesson learned about the conduct of amphibious operations that is still applied today—and that is that the force has to be sustainable.

Guadalcanal was one of the epic battles of the war and of Marine history. It lasted six months; the outcome was often in doubt, the fighting ferocious. Japanese attacks across the Tenaru river ground to a halt against the Marine foxholes and machine gun positions, were chopped to pieces, shattered, and repulsed with Japanese and Marine dead side by side. The Marines' clothes rotted away. They caught all sorts of diseases—and stayed on the line and fought anyway. It was a horrible time, physically and morally for many. They didn't have enough food, information, ammunition. It was the first real offensive ground combat for Americans in the war, after a long

Inchon, Korea. Marines go over the sea wall and into the fields of fire of the enemy. Although the "experts" had pronounced conventional land warfare and amphibious operations obsolete after the introduction of strategic air power and the nuclear bomb, the Korean War corrected conventional wisdom. The Inchon landing was a gamble with high stakes that luckily succeeded. USMC

string of defeats. And even many Marines were unsure if Guadalcanal would be another defeat or the first victory. The Marines were too weak to expand the perimeter and too stubborn to retreat for months. Gradually, they wore out the Japanese, who finally withdrew and escaped with what was left of their forces to try again. It was, after all, a Marine victory—the first in a long, bloody, costly series that would last until 1945.

There were some important lessons learned from the experience. It had been cobbled together, in haste and desperation—there wasn't any choice about that. But Operation Shoestring revealed how vulnerable a task force could be without reliable logistic support

115

Col Lewis B. "Chesty" Puller (left) confers with Brig Gen E. A. Craig during the push to the Korean capital of Seoul on 25 September 1950. USMC by Sgt William Compton

and that the logistic support needed reliable air cover. The Marine landing on Guadalcanal succeeded despite the lack of those components, but it was a warning. The Marines and other American forces in the Pacific had its first stepping stone; there were plenty more to be taken.

With a secure base, the campaign began. Marine task forces began taking islands, moving around others, crawling toward Japan. From Guadalcanal it was just a short hop to New Georgia—the assault went across the beach on 21 February 1943. It was the same old story of fanatical resistance and harsh, jungle climate, but now there was better resupply and air cover from the new F4U Corsairs and the older Wildcats.

Bougainville was next, then Cape Gloucester, then the little atoll called Tarawa.

Tarawa

Okay, so there are no guarantees in war—but it was worse than it should have been. The Navy knew that the tides were tricky around the Gilberts, but Adm. Kelly Turner took a chance on them at Tarawa. On 20 November 1943 he sent the Marines ashore knowing there was a chance that the tide would be low. It was.

The first waves went in aboard Landing Vehicles, Tracked (LVTs), landing craft with tank-like tracks, also called Amtracks. They got over the reefs and put the Marines on the beach, Japanese bullets pinging off the hulls. But the follow-on force were in conventional landing craft called Higgins boats; they got to the coral reef and no farther. Marines "unassed" the boats and headed for the distant beach, hundreds of meters away. Between the intense Japanese machine-gun fire and the uneven bottom, about half made it. When the tide finally came in, it brought dead Marines with it and left them at the high water mark.

Before the invasion, the Japanese commander had said, "A million men cannot take Tarawa in a hundred years." It took about 5,500 Marines three days, but about 1,000 of them died in the process, another 2,000 wounded—50 percent casualties. They called it "Terrible Tarawa." Another lesson learned.

The lesson was applied after Tarawa. Kwajalien was next; the Navy donated artillery rounds to the Japanese for two months. While that removed a bit of the surprise element to the assault, it did a lot more to reduce the defenses. And the Navy was a lot more careful about beach surveys and landing-craft employment. This time, against a bigger garrison, the casualties were a third of Tarawa's.

Peleliu, 15 September 1944: 1st Marine Division attacked this small Japanese garrison, one of the stepping stones to the Philippines and ultimately Japan. The battle was not expected to be especially difficult. Just after first light the 1st, 5th, and 7th Marine

Regiments landed abreast on the western side of the island. The 1st Marines were lightly engaged coming ashore but then hit heavy defenses just across the beach and went to ground; twenty-six of their Amtracks were shattered in the surf. The 5th Marines went ashore near the airfield, and quickly seized it.

Then the Japanese counterattacked with an armor-infantry force across the airfield. The tanks were destroyed by the Marine 37mm anti-tank guns and the M4 Sherman tanks that had made it ashore. By the end of the day, over 1,100 Marines were casualties, 210 of them dead.

The island was riddled with caves that had been developed into defensive, mutually supporting positions. The Marines took them, one hole at a time. Death Valley and Bloody Nose became part of the heritage of the Corps.

At Hill 100 Capt Everett Pope worked his little Company C, 1/1, around the back of the hill where the defenses were lighter, surprised the Japanese and gained the top. They held all night, fighting until their ammunition was gone—then they fought with rocks and ammo boxes. At the end, Pope had fifteen Marines left, but he still had the hill. Later, they gave him a Medal of Honor.

After a week of combat 1st Marines took more than 50 percent casualties—almost 4,000 Marines. Reinforcements arrived from the Army, elements of the 81st Infantry Division, and the attack continued. Marine F4U Corsairs provided close air support for 5th and 7th Marine Regiments; the regiment names were still the same but most of the men and equipment had been replaced, the hard way. A month after the Marines came ashore, the di-

The 1903 Springfield rifle was still the weapon of choice half a century after its introduction. Lt Fred Tees is using this one to annoy enemy troops foolish enough to expose themselves to his fire near the Seoul River bridge. Seoul, Korea, 1950. USMC

Too damn close for comfort, a well-aimed enemy 82mm mortar round lands on a Marine position in Korea, 1952. USMC by E. A. McDade

Dug in on the exposed crest of a Korean ridge, another M46 fires at a distant target, scattering snow.

the operation. With their air cover gone, the Japanese Navy was suddenly vulnerable to air strikes and lost three carriers while trying to withdraw.

Ashore, nearly 29,000 Japanese were killed and about 1,000 were captured by Marines and soldiers; American losses were high, too, with 3,426 killed in action.

On 21 July, the 3rd Marine Division, III Marine Amphibious Corps, and the 77th US Army Division stormed the shores of Guam. Here, and it seemed everywhere else, Japanese "Banzai" attacks came any time, anywhere. Company cooks, clerks, and anybody else were suddenly called on to grab a rifle and help fend off a few hundred frenzied enemy coming through the wire. The Japanese attacks were violent in the extreme. There was no time to prepare. Marines had to respond immediately, effectively. They did it with old 1903 Springfield rifles, with knives, and with shovels when it came to that. But the rifle did the most killing, even in the hands of a cook or clerk. Another lesson learned.

Iwo Jima

If you've got to fight, try not to do it on a place like Iwo Jima. The island was one big natural obstacle. Soft sand and ash made walking difficult. Wheels and tracks slid and spun in it. Farther inland, a maze of well-placed defensive positions, all mutually supporting, with interlocking fields of fire, commanded the beaches and beyond. Despite an extensive bombardment by naval gunfire before the Marine landing on 19 February 1945, the island had to be taken an inch at a time, paid for in Marine blood. About 21,000 Americans, mostly Marines, were casualties on Iwo, and 6,821 were killed. As Lt Gen. H. M. ("Howling Mad") Smith commented, "The fighting was the toughest the Marines ran across in 168 years."

When the task forces slowly closed the noose on Japan two things happened: the resistance stiffened and the Navy/Marine team polished the amphibious operation to a fine art. By the time Okinawa was assaulted, the

vision was relieved by the Army to complete the mopping up. Peleliu cost 1st Marine Division 1,241 killed, 5,024 wounded, and 117 missing. Eight Medals of Honor were later presented to Marines who fought on the island. Of the Japanese garrison of over 10,000 only about 300 survived, all captured.

The Great Marianas Turkey Shoot

On 15 June 1944, the Normandy invasion of Europe had been getting all the headlines, but out in the Marianas Islands, Marines were going ashore again, this time against 30,000 Japanese on Saipan. If you wonder why Marines place so much emphasis on the combat-air-patrol mission, Saipan has something to do with it.

No sooner was the force ashore than the Japanese Navy showed up, full of fight. In a transparent sky, Marine and Japanese fighters fought it out in what became known as The Great Marianas Turkey Shoot. Five hundred combat aircraft went down to the massed fires of Marine and Navy fighters and to the gunfire of the 535 US Navy ships supporting

kind of fumbles that wasted lives at Guadalcanal and Tarawa were pretty much a thing of the past. Even so, Okinawa cost 5,000 American lives, soldiers and Marines.

Korea

When it was time for Marines to go to war again, in 1950, it was in the traditional way—badly unprepared. Korea was the war that wasn't supposed to happen. After the development of the atomic bomb, politicians and planners decided that amphibious operations and conventional infantry campaigns were a thing of the past. The North Korean Army had other ideas and came storming across the 38th Parallel on 25 June 1950, seven divisions of infantry and one of armor.

There were only about 80,000 Marines on active duty, and few of those were dedicated to the Fleet Marine Forces. The United States attempted to reinvent, in a couple of desperate weeks, all that had been discarded after the war. Reservists were called up, and a hasty, stop-gap force was launched into the breach.

If the fighting in the Pacific had been ghastly, Korea was worse. It was the acid test of the Corps in a way that even Tarawa and Peleliu were not. There, you could simply be shot and die; in Korea you had to march, freeze, climb hills, go without sleep, and—perhaps the worst—do it all with other US and United Nations forces fleeing in panic all around you. Then you could die.

The amphibious assault was a mission that was supposed to never be needed again, so the ships were discarded along with most of the doctrine in the postwar era. Suddenly, the Marines were supposed to do it again at Inchon—this time with only a couple of weeks to prepare, without the Landing Ship, Tanks (LSTs), and against a beach with thirty-foot tides. The landing was pulled off, by luck, audacity, and scrounged landing craft. The landing at Inchon didn't win the war but it prevented defeat, for the moment.

As it was supposed to do, the landing and lodgment shocked the North Korean command and the enemy recoiled, vulnerable. Then,

suddenly, it was a rout and the enemy force collapsed, running for the north or dying in place.

Then, just when everybody was getting complacent again, the Chinese Army joined the fight and suddenly there was another ordeal by fire and ice at Chosin Reservoir. There, in November and December 1950, the 1st Marine Division, particularly the 5th and 7th Marine Regiments, bled again. They conducted one of the most gallant fighting withdrawals in American history, bringing their frozen dead with them.

In the end, the war was concluded without victory or defeat, after 4,262 Marines had died

Grenada, 1983. These Marines have come ashore by helicopter from the USS Guam and will shortly move out to begin securing the town. The Guam had been en route to Lebanon and was diverted to participate in the attack. When it was over, the Marines re-embarked and proceeded with the original mission. USMC

The air-ground team in action. A CH-46 pulls pitch, departing a lonely outpost before the Gulf ground war kicked off. In the foreground is an LAV-25 (Light Armored Vehicle) that has managed to gather a crowd. USMC/Maj Mark Hughes

and almost 22,000 had been wounded. The numbers were about double those for World War I, yet without the honors or the successful conclusion. When the shooting stopped, the line between North and South was right back where it had been at the outset.

Vietnam

Marines first went to Vietnam in 1962 when Medium Helicopter Squadron 362 set up shop at Soc Trang in the Mekong Delta. The squadron flew H-34 helicopters, supporting Vietnamese infantry units by delivering them to previously inaccessible areas of operation. Marine ground operations got underway in 1965, but the Marine talents and training for rapid, offensive, amphibious assaults were ignored by a National Command Authority that never really figured out just what the mission was supposed to be.

Marines demonstrated that the old Semper Fi intensity was still SOP, but it was largely wasted at places like Khe Sahn in static, defensive battles with little strategic purpose.

Grenada, Panama, and Southwest Asia

In the years after the Vietnam War concluded, Marines have been detailed to many of the same kinds of expeditions as they always have, and often to the same places. The Grenada operation, Urgent Fury, demonstrated the effectiveness and efficiency of the Marine way of conducting business. While the Army's Rangers and Airborne were having some difficulty completing their D-day missions, the Marines (who were detoured from a

trip to Lebanon) executed theirs with speed and a businesslike dispatch—then backloaded on the ships and went off to the Mediterranean.

The Gulf war was interesting to Marine historians and policymakers less for the valor displayed on the battlefield than the way the Corps functioned. Few of the Marines sent to (as they now call it) southwest Asia (SWA) had combat experience. The MPS (Maritime Pre-Positioning Ships) idea hadn't been tested. Neither had most of the vehicles, aircraft, weapons, or support systems, outside of training. After decades of anticipating a conflict with the Soviet Union or a surrogate, probably in Northern Europe, the US armed forces suddenly found themselves with a completely different problem to solve. But SWA didn't look a lot different to Marines than their training grounds at Twentynine Palms, without the lumps.

The MPS concept was fully validated, although the six-month buildup was conducted without any opposition. The Marines were feeding the Army and Air Force for a while at the beginning of operations because the other services' supplies hadn't caught up with the troops. Offensive operations based on overwhelming firepower, mobility, and technological developments turned out to be spectacularly successful. Although the Gulf war didn't include an opposed amphibious assault, it did test the independent and expeditionary parts of the Marine mission, which managed to confound every skeptic. The consensus of opinion on the Gulf experience is that the Marine Corps was the right package in the right place for the right problem.

Chapter 7

The Future of the Corps

The Marine Corps is a curious institution. It is a small, odd, stubborn, emotional, opinionated congregation of characters and missions. It is a community that reeks of tradition, adores its heroes (living and dead), a place where grown men can talk about love for each other and their institution without apology or explanation. It is a place full of life, dedicated to the business of death and destruction. In an era when sloth and self-indulgence are popular virtues, Marines seek and celebrate opposite values, a dedication to a kind of mental and physical fitness.

Throughout its entire history, 217 years at this writing, this little Corps of Marines has been a little out of step with the larger society it defends—often slandered, frequently threatened, seldom honored, never secure within the federal budget. It has always been a small, exclusive, discriminating club with initiation fees that are far too expensive, in terms of commitment, integrity, and discomfort, for most Americans. Its members are hard in a soft time, cheerful in adversity. By all rights this little Corps should have evaporated years ago, like the Federal Lighthouse Service, forgotten and unmourned—another archaic waste (if you listen to the bean counters) of

Sergeant Bopp works in the division communication section. She's been living in a tent at Twentynine Palms lovely guest facility, Camp Wilson, for a month now and somehow still manages to be cheerful about it.

On 10 November every year Marines wherever they are celebrate the birthday of their Corps with formal ceremonies and informal gatherings.

123

Each decoration tells a story: He was wounded in combat twice, cited for valor by the Navy, awarded the Vietnamese Cross of Gallantry, served several tours in Southeast Asia; he qualified as a parachutist and fired expert with the rifle and sharpshooter with the pistol. He stood on this parade deck about the time these recruits were born, stood in the same ranks, learned the same lessons, took them to combat and stayed in the Corps to carry on the tradition. The first sergeant deserves to be called "sir."

Capt Carl E. Mundy III commands Bravo Company, 1/9. His helmet has been adorned with a scrap of camouflage netting to break up the visual outline. It is called (among other things) the "Tina Turner" look.

taxpayer's money. Instead, the institution and its inmates have thrived on all the adversity that the fates and fortunes of the passage of time have provided.

Once again there is discussion of abolishing the Marine Corps or shrinking it to invisibility, using the money for something else more politically correct. That is certainly the American tradition, and perhaps it will come to pass. The bigger services could certainly absorb the missions of the Marines, and do most of them in a professional manner. With the demise of the Warsaw Pact threat, there isn't much left for the Air Force, Army, and Navy to keep themselves busy, and some politicians have been hinting again that maybe the Marine Corps is a waste of money.

Well, one Marine officer, Major Peterson recently came up with an intriguing alternative idea: Instead of abolishing the Marine Corps, why not get rid of the Army, Navy, and Air Force . . . and keep the Marine Corps? Why not indeed. About the only service whose mission is likely to remain unchanged is this little expeditionary force, naval in character, task-organized for each individual operation, agile, and self-sustaining. Perhaps there is a future for selected parts of the Army, Air Force, and Navy—as components of the Marine Air-Ground Task Force.

While the bigger services try to sort out just what their mission is on the battlefields of the future, Marines already know about theirs. It it the same mission it has always been, the one Presley O'Bannon and his motley crew had in 1805 and that will be around for Marines forever. Marines know that, in a month or a year, there will be hostages to save, an insurrection to put down, a revolution or coup to suppress, a war to be won. They

The M249 Squad Automatic Weapon (SAW) is a light, compact, reliable support weapon that puts a lot of suppressive fire on an objective during the assault. It uses the same ammunition as the M16 rifle, either in magazines or 250-round plastic assault packs.

Whatever becomes of the Marine Corps in the future, some things will never change—the haircuts, the inspections, and the character of the officers and enlisted Marines.

know that, sooner or later, the orders will trickle down the chain of command, from the president on high to the commanders of the expeditionary forces. The plans will be made, the orders and ammunition issued. A Marine task force will move across the seas. On some dark future night, off a beach whose name we don't yet know, Marines with rifles will nervously wait for their leaders to lead them

ashore. They will mount up on the LAVs and AAVs and helicopters. At the appointed hour, the force will be launched at some distant, hostile shore. Marines, just as they have for well over 200 years, will rush across the fire-swept beaches and inland toward their objectives. They will accomplish their mission, at whatever cost, bring their dead and wounded with them—just like always. Semper Fi.

The Marine Hymn

From the halls of Montezuma
   To the shores of Tripoli
We fight our country's battles
   In the air, on land and sea.
First to fight for right and freedom,
   And to keep our honor clean,
We are proud to claim the title
   Of United States Marines.
Our flag's unfurl'd to every breeze
   From dawn to setting sun;
We have fought in every clime and place
   Where we could take a gun.

In the snow of far-off northern lands
   And in sunny tropic scenes,
You will always find us on the job—
   The United States Marines.
Here's health to you and to our Corps
   Which we are proud to serve;
In many a strife we've fought for life
   And never lost our nerve.
If the Army and the Navy
   Ever gaze on heaven's scenes,
They will find the streets are guarded
   By United States Marines.

Honors and Campaigns

Revolutionary War, 1775–1783
Quasi-War with France, 1798–1801
Barbary Wars, 1801–1815
War of 1812, 1812–1815
African Slave Trade Patrol, 1820–1861
Indian Wars, 1811–1812; 1836–1842
Operations Against West Indian Pirates,
   1822–1830
Mexican War, 1846–1848
Civil War, 1861–1865

Spanish Campaign, 1898
Philippine Campaign, 1899–1904
China Relief Expedition, 1900–1901
Cuban Pacification, 1906–1909
Nicaraguan Campaign, 1912
Mexican Service, 1914
Haitian Campaign, 1915; 1919–1920
Dominican Campaign, 1916
World War I, 1917–1918
Army of Occupation, 1918–1923

Second Nicaraguan Campaign, 1926–1933
Yangtze Service, 1926–1927; 1930–1932
China Service, 1937–1939; 1945–1947
American Defense Service, 1939–1941
American Campaign, 1941–1946
European-African-Middle Eastern
    Campaign, 1941–1945
Asiatic-Pacific Campaign, 1941–1946
World War II Victory, 1941–1946
Navy Occupation Service, 1945–1955
National Defense Service, 1950–1954;
    1961–1974
Korean Service, 1950–1954
Armed Forces Expeditionary, 1958–1975

Vietnam Service, 1962–1973
French Croix de Guerre, 1918
Philippine Defense, 1941–1942
Philippine Liberation, 1944–1945
Philippine Independence, 1941–1945
Philippine Presidential Unit Citation,
    1950–1954
Korean Presidential Unit Citation,
    1950–1954
Republic of Vietnam Meritorious Unit
    Citation of the Gallantry Cross with
    Palm, 1965–1969
Republic of Vietnam Meritorious Unit
    Citation, Civil Actions, 1969–1970

US Marine Corps Battle Deaths
(major conflicts only)

Revolutionary War: 49
War of 1812: 45
Mexican War: 11
Civil War (Union side only): 148
Spanish-American War: 6

World War I: 2,461
World War II: 19,733
Korean War: 1,302
Vietnam: 13,082

Index